Sail On

Savannah Ugan

DEDICATION

To all who have gone before us, braving the oceans to find new lands. To the ones who built bridges over raging waters and expansive chasms for our safety and ease. To my grandparents, parents, pastors, mentors, and friends who have done that and more for me. I am grateful.

CONTENTS

CONTENTS

PREFACE

I opened the weighty door of a hospital room, and my
world began to spin. Laying on the bed in front of me was a
smaller, more fragile version of my grandpa than the one who
spent the summer before showing me around Sacramento. I knew
what I would be walking into, so I can't say what caught me so off
guard. The smell of the hospital overwhelmed me. I became acutely
aware of discarded needles boxed on the wall and how high we
were in the building.

I sat on the couch by the window and noticed all the family
albums on the table before me. Seconds after cracking one open, I
set it back down. Too many good memories in those pages hid
from the somberness of the moment; I didn't want to spoil them.
The present felt painful. I would give anything for his cheeks to fill
out and his face to have color again.

His slow breaths continued for two more sweet, heart-
wrenching weeks until he made it Home. I don't know why that
memory stuck with me among all the bitter and sweet during his

battle with cancer. He consistently influenced my life with a sense of belonging and support. When times were good, he celebrated with me. When times were rough, we found ways to laugh at my misfortunes. When times were sad, he would encourage me with the classic lyrics of Simon and Garfunkel:

Sail on, silver girl
Sail on by
Your time has come to shine
All your dreams are on their way
See how they shine
If you need a friend
I'm sailing right behind
Like a bridge over troubled water
I will ease your mind

Years have passed since I felt that great divide between heaven and earth. I remember fondly what it's like to have someone be my bridge over troubled waters. I know what it's like to be a bridge for someone afraid of drowning in the terrors of this life. I hope to ease your mind with the same love and lessons that have carried me down the river of life.

This labor of love is a collection of thoughts on perseverance through loss, grief, dreams, accomplishments, and, most dearly, love. These pages contain years of discoveries, carefully considered and selectively shared. Aside from publishing my journal, my best efforts to be transparently authentic lie within the coming chapters for your consideration. As you read through, I pray you are inspired, challenged, and rebuilt to be more resilient than before. In all this, I have learned everything comes down to persevering love.

LESSON 1

The cap on my oxytocin must be loose in my brain because I feel those warm, loving chemicals toward nearly anything big-eyed and breathing. My dog is the primary target. When I saw that baby rottweiler mutt on a rescue site, I knew he would be mine. I drove seven hours to North Carolina and back to adopt him the day after finding his picture online. The rescue site had named him Carver, but I changed it to John Tyree after a character in one of my favorite romance novels: *Dear John*. John Tyree became Ty and is now most affectionately "Tyty." The name changes did not stop there. Eventually, though, I simply called him "Mine."

"Mine" became a pet name for more than just my pet. Like a toddler with her toys, I began to call friends "Mine." I like to think my friends weren't annoyed; some even appreciated it. Deep below the humor, per usual, was a truth that made me sad. As much as I wish people, things, and places were mine, they are not.

In just a few decades, I've learned that many people we love won't be along for the whole ride. I have a hard time persevering through loss. Sometimes, welcoming people close to my heart can be painful, especially with all the memories of those left behind. It seems that's a cost of love: cherishing memories and letting go.

Looking around me, I recognize that nothing I have is mine. Any moment, even right now, I could lose anything I hold dear. My possessions could be stolen, lost, or burned. My dog could run off. My friends could lose touch. My favorite clothes could (and will) go out of style. Thinking everything will go away scares me. Thinking back on what and who I used to love feels distant to me. I am disconnected from people who used to be pillars in my life. I hate that life nudges us until we are states, seas, or heavens apart. When I think about losing people in my life, I feel the weight of fear. The grief of losing my grandpa gave voice to my fears in a louder way. My brain worked to predict the future and self-preserve. With all the pain I felt from a recent loss, fear naturally built. I could repress that fear. I could find ways to coexist with it. Instead, I presented those fears to God, trusting He is my Comforter.

I peered through the potential and inevitable losses ahead of me. My mind wanted to create a narrative that I would lose the people I love. This is when I "look at the negative space." Coming from a family of artists, I know that the focus of a masterpiece isn't always the most prominent object. The empty space around it, the negative space, can be just as important. The prominent object I see is loss. Looking around, I see bonds of attachment I've been blessed to create with people. I have ample opportunities to love and be loved by people. God has connected us to loved ones, new friends, and strangers. The possibility of love is as close as the person nearest to me.

God designed an intricately beautiful life system in which our bodies come from dust and return to dust. Death is a part of life here. As scary as it feels, death is not something we have to live in fear of. We can find purpose in our days, knowing they are finite and not meant to persist here forever. We can connect with others around us who are in the same boat. We were somehow purposefully birthed into the same era, stories intertwining. Exorbitant potential exists in the endless combinations of relationships to be formed.

In a society where playing relationship games with one another is the norm, we have the freedom to put aside social scripts and follow the example of Jesus. We can choose refreshing honesty when mystery is expected. We can provide from the Source of love instead of our limited internal sources of attachment and attraction. We aren't separate from humanity, but we are hosts of divinity. The love that created us is eternal, not confined by trust issues and fear of abandonment. This love is not selfish and impatient. God's example of love is hopeful, generous, and freely given to us.

As I prayed one afternoon, I closed my eyes and asked God how in tune with love I was. The imagery of water came to mind. Was love a small, continuous drip I tried to ignore because the stress of life had me preoccupied? Was love a storm I watched from my window alone, witnessing the power of it over others but feeling distanced from it myself? Was love a spring of freshwater flowing for the refreshment of the thirsty? Regardless of if I feel little or much, love is always present. Walls we put up in our hearts may stifle or confine the love that would normally be able to flow freely. Love releases as we let go of barriers we've constructed out of fear. Boundaries are riverbeds and shorelines; we want to keep them in place. But fear, insecurity, and bitterness clog the natural movement of love in us.

One evening, I curled up on my couch with my oversized blanket and turned on *The Time Traveler's Wife*. Toward the end, Rachel McAdams' character hears her husband has reappeared. She drops everything she is doing to run to him. She is racing through the forest, hoping she does not miss him. They reunite in a powerfully tender embrace just in time. And just as quickly, he disappears. The look on her face said everything. She encapsulates the familiarity of loss in an expression so devastated yet understood. The times I've felt that resurfaced. Moments come and go. We get to feel the pleasure of being with someone we love and the pain of losing someone we love. Rarely could anyone ever experience one without the other.

4

Losing someone to conflict, illness, death, distance, and all the other difficulties in the world hurts. My natural tendencies pendulum swing between controlling or hiding from everyone to avoid feeling the sting of loss. Those are no ways to live and, certainly, no ways to love.

Even when loss could be the outcome, am I the friend who drops everything to run and embrace someone? That is how I want to love people: fearlessly, hopefully, presently. I hope for the courage to accept every moment of love I can give to or receive from strangers, friends, family, and God.

I know God's love to be fearless and hopeful. He is engaged in my life and present in my experiences. I want to love Him back that way. He would see me running toward the sound of Him, dropping everything to get to Him. How would life be different if we loved God and others like that? Not recklessly but generously expressing the gratitude we feel toward each other. That is a possibility when the love of God begins to dilute and cycle out our own selfish, "Mine" sort of love.

I won't bring people into freedom with selfish love; I will have them in possession. This can constrict their identity, purpose, trust, and peace. Self-serving love is no real love at all. Instead, I release possession of the ones I love and trust God. With God as my Source, I engage in behaviors similar to before but with entirely different motives. Texting friends is about connecting with them, not filling a void for attention. Talking to strangers is about

5

showing kindness, not seeking something to gain. Going to church is about what I can give, not get. This kind of love can only come from believing God loves us first.

God so loved the world that He gave His life. That is the invitation for us. We can offer our lives, too. We give ourselves not to be loved but to love. No more expectations to meet, approval to gain, or attention to attract. Sometimes, I need a hard reset to stop straining for my needs to be met under the facade of selfish love. Loving with my hands wide open may feel like a struggle, but that is the best way to allow life to thrive. I don't want to squeeze the life out of what I have. I would rather watch it move and breathe. I want to nurture life's growth.

In this life, loss is a strong possibility, and love is a risky business. I must refuse to give into, live, or act from fear because fear traps me in self-interest. Fear tempts me to focus on my wants and needs to make me feel okay again. Times may get scary and hurt, but I choose not to live afraid.

A hard truth I grapple with is that God lets people He loves die. He let Lazarus die. He let Jesus die. The father in the Gospel story was actively pursuing Jesus, and God let his daughter die. What happened after these earthly resurrections? Did Mary and Martha watch Lazarus die all over again later in life? Did the man's daughter become ill again? One of the most reliable, innately human, universal experiences is death.

When I sat at the bedside of my dying grandfather while cancer tore his body apart, I felt profound love. I felt an emotion so strongly I could not find the word for it. A blend of comfort, fear, thankfulness, closeness, emptiness, and hope raged inside me. The power of those emotions lived in my body and brought tears to my eyes.

I said goodbye, not knowing if he could hear me. My hand held onto his, though he couldn't hold on back. I cried, and he couldn't open his eyes to know I was there. The uneasy relief of a closed chapter accompanied me on the ride home. Then the devastation hit, and I cried alone in bed in an acute realization that our closeness was severed. Behind my immediate pain lurked the thought of all the other people he left behind, all the other people who are dying of cancer, and all of the moments in my future he won't be there for.

Exhaustion hit, and I lay still while tears streamed down my tired face. That's when the darkness hit. The world was different. That's when I found myself in the presence of my Comforter, but feeling anger and bitterness like never before. There would be a lot to unpack in the days ahead. The process of healing would take a long time. As you might have guessed, God was never at fault. He is and has been and will be Love. God is not selfishly, fearfully loving. He is self-controlled and wisely loving. I just couldn't see the truth through my tears initially.

Yes, we were born from dust and will return to it. My emotions like to intrude on the simplicity of that truth. But this is one of the many reasons I love Jesus: He is life. He is Resurrection power. He does not cower away from death. He holds the keys to death.

The sound of Jesus' name on our lips is powerful. Speaking that Word, calling His attention, changes things. Jesus' name is power, provision, protection, and peace. We ask in His name, and He responds to show us the Father's great love. He, Three-in-One, is for us. I recall the testimonies of His faithfulness in my life, and I am encouraged that He will continue to be faithful. Jesus keeps my fears of death far away.

I hate to be morbid, but I want to normalize this conversation. One day, my sweet Ty will die, and I will be sad. One day, I will die, and people will be sad. But I have complete confidence that I will never lose my life. When my body fails, my spirit will rest and rejoice in an eternity of love. In the light of eternity, death is a shadow laid down behind us; our spirits persist. So, until I die, I am committed and determined to love. And when I die, I will be ready and eager to love forever in an even better way.

LESSON 2

Do you ever have a day that is just plain good? Let me tell you about one of mine. I slept in until about 8:30 (which is late for me) because I stayed up past midnight watching movies the night before with a friend. I walked my dog and fed him. I had the nail salon to myself for the first half hour of my appointment. My regular nail tech came in late, so she gave me a massage with my fresh, clean, funny-bunny nails. I decided to go wild at Kroger. I purchased the fixings for some great meals: balsamic pear pizza, date chicken over pasta, chili peanut chicken with egg noodles, tostones and mojo, and brie grilled cheese with a mango jalapeno jam.

Cooking up the tostones sounded like a quick, enjoyable brunch. I plated them using my smallest charcuterie board and a ¼ cup clay measuring cup for the mojo. All the while, my candles were burning, and soft music filled my little condo. I threw all the dishes in the sink because I don't like doing dishes. The hour before my class started, I took a solid nap. Minutes into class, my professor let us out hours early for self-care. I headed to the Starbucks on Hammond Drive with my laptop and current book. These Starbucks employees are excellent greeters, making my dog seem like a local celebrity as they deliver his usual order: a shot-sized *puppuccino*. I snagged my cold brew from the counter and found a shady spot on the patio.

I sat criss-crossed on a bench outside, guarded by my content pup and embracing the cool breeze in the warm weather. All those little moments, all stitched together, made for a great day. I hadn't planned it, but I got it. I rolled with what came along, and it was beautiful.

If you're like me, you pile your plate up high. I had graduate school, a job, another job, a dog to keep alive, a house to keep clean, and a self to care for. In addition to the basics, I had family, friends, and hobbies to keep up with. Laidback days are precious gifts, pretty few and far between.

Days like that remind me of the simple truth that God is good. He is good, and He loves to give us good things. This is not always easy to believe, but that does not make it less true. Being still helps me to see the good gifts He has given me. This puts a whole new spin on His call for us to be still and know Him. Our stillness can lead us to recognize His engagement in our lives.

Lately, I have been the loudest advocate that God works all things together for our good. I had decided to pause my education with graduate school and pursue full-time ministry. This massive, unexpected change felt peaceful and natural. More than anything, I felt relief. Having ended school but not yet started a full-time position in ministry, I had plenty of time to reflect. I had been going through old journals, discovering the thread of God's purpose for me in all I have experienced. I'm amazed by how the pieces have fallen into place.

In a journal entry from July 2020, I wrote about my anxiety about moving to Atlanta from Athens. I had dreamed of moving to Sacramento but hit several setbacks. The setbacks did not make that move impossible, but they did make it difficult enough for me to pause and consider what I wanted to do moving forward. Atlanta seemed like the way to go. I worked at the eye doctor across the street from my condo and lived alone for the first few weeks. As a highly extroverted little lady, I did not enjoy my office job or being alone so much. I had two friends in Atlanta who lived twenty minutes away and kept busy with their full-time jobs. Starting graduate school had stressed me more than I hoped it would.

All those fears and steps forward seem distant now. I had no idea I would eventually pause my education after my first year of school so I could return to ministry. I couldn't have anticipated the setbacks that allowed me to reconsider what I wanted. I spent a week praying about my hesitations and hopes for my job and future. I had expected the familiar feelings of betrayal, confusion, and mistrust toward God when things didn't turn out my way. But I felt peacefully confident in His love for me. This confidence was a remarkable sign of healing in me. I had been bruised and bloody for a long time over disappointments from my past. Reading through my journals showed me how much the Lord had recovered in me. I didn't know how far I had come until I took the time to pause. Gratitude welled up in me.

How we respond to stillness indicates the state of our inner world. Stillness reveals our exhaustion, discomfort, growth, and peace. When I hesitate to rest because I don't want to be alone with my thoughts, I can safely assume something is off. When I only have the energy to sleep in stillness and wake up feeling tired anyway, I know my rest is not producing peace. When I am still and feel accomplished or God's pleasure over what I've done, that's a mark of growth.

This is my testimony. For a long time, I wrestled with God. I fought and screamed and cried. I felt the crippling fear and deep hopelessness of not knowing what to believe about God when my experiences did not align with what I thought He was like. Over and over and over, I drew near to Him because I wanted to know the truth. "God, why does this still hurt? How could You let this happen? Why didn't you warn me? Do I have a say in what happens around me?" Endless questions streamed from my spirit as I held onto the conviction that He would answer with great, unsearchable things I didn't know yet. Just like He promised, He drew near to me.

The healing slowly flowed through the time we spent together. Reading a chapter or two in the Bible each night challenged my misconceptions of Him and grounded me in truth. Journaling prayers provided accountability for what I asked for and what I felt like He was saying in return. Praying through memories brought me face-to-face with the disappointments of the past so I might reconcile them with the hope of Christ. I could count on one hand the moments of healing that felt glamorous. I felt irrational joy for a few weeks in a year of ugly mess. The love between God and me was undeniably real. I would be beaming with the latest thing He taught me, feasting on the fruit of His Spirit in me. The rest of the time, life felt fine or slightly less than. The fact of the matter is that feelings aren't God. Feelings can be deceptive; feelings can lead us to believe that we are so much farther from our breakthroughs and wholeness than we hope. Being with God aligns us back with the truth. He is working all things together for our good.

I had expected one thing, and God did another. Not only can I see now that His plan was better than mine, but He had every right to because He's God. At some point, we have to stop agreeing with the lie we know best. It's not every man for himself down here. We have a Father who loves us and wants to care for us. I had braced for another year of toiling and struggling, but He brought relief surprisingly soon. My career had shifted to a new direction in a matter of days. I would not have taken advantage of the opportunity for change without the disruption that caused me to pause. Obstacles and barriers are not impossible for us to move past, but we need to know we're fighting the battles we want to fight before throwing our lives out on the line. Perhaps a clearer pathway is closer than you think.

Take the Israelites, for example. They could have fought the Philistines on the way to the promised land. Maybe they would have won; maybe they would have been enslaved or killed. Instead, they went to the sea, where God created a clearer path. This is the same God we abide by today. He will lead you into your promised land. You may walk through valleys of death and wildernesses of temptation, but those problematic places are not your destination. And really, even the things you hope for differ from your destination. The destination is eternity with God, who wildly and passionately loves you. Don't lose sight of that; it changes everything.

If you, like me, have hesitations about the fullness of God's love in light of your circumstances, persist. Keep bringing them before God. Trust that you will understand in time. Comfort comes in many ways, more ways than understanding. Let God comfort you how He wants to; I promise He knows you well. There is undeniable truth to His everlasting love for you; believe me. The fruit of His Spirit in you is love. His feelings toward you are love. His gift to you is love. His thoughts about you are love. Nothing can overcome it. Go to Him because He loves you and because you want to. Let Him love you.

Slowing down and pausing allows us to recognize the world around us. We meet strangers and welcome smiles. Slower paces let us pour our love from God into those around us. Just like the Starbucks baristas slow down to make a *puppuccino* for my dog, which makes his day, we can slow down to make someone feel special. We can be kind, but kindness requires intentionality. Be intentional to listen to the Spirit, rest with the Spirit, and live with the Spirit. That's where we can expect transformation to begin in and around us.

Intentionality and consistency come from balance. When we can sustain healthy rhythms, we become more dependable. Slow down, rest, speed up, work. God created us to thrive in rhythms. In a success-driven and anxiety-ridden culture, slowing down to enjoy life is ridiculous. But that's exactly what Jesus invites us to do: abide in Him so our joy may be complete.

The secrets of life are all tucked away in the Word of God. God has relief for you if the life you've been trying to hold together is breaking. God has rest for you. He has life for you. Find your delicious home-cooked meal or take full advantage of unexpected breaks in the day. Be with the ones you love and find safe havens. Show kindness to those around you. This life is too short to run into the ground. You could make it something incredible, something beautiful. Just slowing down won't get you there, but you won't get there without slowing down sometimes. Find your Starbucks on Hammond and enjoy the days.

LESSON 3

I am naturally a systemic thinker. When I discovered how to think analytically, my whole world opened up. I found immense value in breaking life into stages and segments. With this way of thinking, there are endings in sight and beginnings around the corner. For a year, I set monthly goals spiritually, emotionally, mentally, physically, socially, occupationally, and financially. The resulting rhythms of life were well worth the effort.

Devoting my full attention to each thing I'm a part of during the time I'm a part of it makes life more cohesive in the long run. It turns out I didn't need to multitask or switch tasks as much as I had been. By cutting out other things, I increased my ability to be present. I didn't have a thousand things cluttering my mind and to-do lists.

Like too many tabs open on a computer, we don't function as well when we have too much going on. We set apart everything that is not immediately required of us and give our energy to that. We limit what we commit to and are involved in to align our capacity and workload. Adjusting this boundary is painful and awkward, but the result is incredibly fruitful.

We feel constantly behind or overwhelmed because we don't cut back the pieces of our lives that need to go. We overcommit and squeeze things in when we could be letting something go and resting between what we feel called to do. This requires discernment. Often, we won't know what is holding us back until we take a step back and survey the busyness we have accumulated. We can see the mess before us and begin organizing it into groups, determining the value and timing, and releasing what needs to be removed.

When we rush through things, we often rush past things. Participating in things when we'd rather be elsewhere distracts us from what is in front of us. We might miss things altogether when our plates get too full. People whose schedules are overcrowded are the ones double-booking, backing out, or showing up distracted. Interactions become transactions rather than transformations. I hope to be ever-evolving into someone better through the things I give my time to.

When I pursued my certificate in Emotional Intelligence back in 2017, my instructor had me take an emotional quotient assessment. My lowest skill was problem-solving. Problem-solving, as defined by the Emotional Intelligence inventory, is the ability to find viable solutions to problems that arise without being overwhelmed by emotion. I naturally tend toward anxiety, which has the opposite effect. My first step to becoming a better problem solver was to break problems into small parts.

This advice is my lifeboat. In my most recent move, I felt initially overwhelmed. Moving uncovers the depth and intensity of our hoarding habits, sentimental or otherwise. Putting my training into place, I dedicated a week to each room in my house. I would throw out, give away, or pack up whatever was in the room of the week, then rest with the time left over. The task felt manageable, and I chipped away at my responsibilities on time. I accomplished everything I needed to, bagging up my anxieties with the rest of the old things I didn't want to bring into my new home.

Breaking things apart is helpful in relationships as well. When conflict muddies our perceptions of people and situations, a little organization can bring a lot of clarity. Maybe a passing comment someone made changed your view of them. Let's break it down. Was their phrasing hurtful, or did it hit a nerve in you? Has the person changed, or are you just seeing more of them? Have they changed, or are you dramatizing because you feel attacked? Was the comment a regrettable moment that can be reconciled or a fundamental block that you may need to work to get around? Parsing heated moments into smaller interactions can help us de-escalate tension.

Sometimes, journaling helps me break things down. One by one, I identify the fears and potential outcomes of a conflict. Then, I weigh the fears with rationality based on our strengths, weaknesses, and character. This isn't meant to be extra work. It's just a system I've created to channel the fog of fears into confidence for how I want to move forward.

At work, I'm sending teams on trips around the world. I had never been in charge of something this huge and expensive. Starting the process felt like a huge question mark. But I broke down mission trips into team care, funding, communication, and so on until I could see the moving parts in front of me. I listed deadlines for each item in each category. My work fell into place, and my full attention went to whatever was required in a given moment.

Breaking our life into bits reminds me of the universe's makeup. Everything we see, touch, smell, taste, and hear can be broken down to the barest of elements. We don't need to tear apart our lives literally. Simply discovering what components make up our lives can be enough. From there, we have the insight we need to make informed decisions about how we want to live.

Breaking life into bits may seem disjointed or detrimental, but it can help us preserve parts of ourselves. We are more capable of memorizing smaller chunks of information. We divide books into chapters, songs into verses, and poems into stanzas. Smaller pieces can be more manageable to safeguard.

Part of me loved watching my dad perform surgery when I was younger. I can recall that part of myself when I get queasy before lab work, confronting the medical phobia I acquired. Part of me spent time on a farm as a girl. A little walk in nature usually does the trick when I'm stressed. I become more well-rounded when I keep those parts of myself intact rather than letting them blend in a distant conglomerate of memory.

Unfortunately, we have parts of ourselves that we would rather forget. The times we suffer or have caused others to suffer are challenging to come to terms with. They feel like they don't belong in my story or like I was a different person then. How we view these fragments of our history is important and will likely change over time as we pursue healing.

During my first year of ministry, a leader had our team write out our stories. We marked a timeline with significant life events and wrote short commentaries on how those events affected us. I felt strange looking at a chronological recollection of my life. Was that really me? Are all those things really what made me the woman I am today? Some parts of my life feel like a different person. Years later, a therapist asked me to recount my story. She illustrated my life as a path as I dictated my history. For each event I recalled, she asked me to assign a rock or rose to that part of the path. The stones represented moments I experienced negatively, and the roses testified to fond memories. My timeline covered all the same material from the first exercise (plus a little of the recent developments), but how I perceived some events had changed. Some of the major disappointments from my first recollection were less significant when looking at them the second time around. Some of the small pleasant moments I had aged to be more sweet and sentimental.

When we repress or deny the parts of our histories that we don't like, we disable ourselves from becoming whole. Chunks of our stories are redacted but hold components of truth that still influence the way we live today. Focusing on the silver lining can break us out of negative thought patterns. To that end, acknowledging the ugly parts of our stories can be an opportunity to learn grace for ourselves and accept the love that covers our mistakes.

The testimony of God's faithfulness to me weaves throughout my history. It's one thing to say God has been good to me. It's another thing to read through the chapters of my life and repeatedly recount His goodness. What are testimonies, if not the pieces of our lives that make His love for us apparent? We have to split up the pieces to get into the specifics of His engagement in our lives. This is who I was. Then, this is who I became because of His grace. This is where I was; then, this is where He brought me because of His mercy. This is what I needed, and that is what He gave me because of His love. With staples like that marking our stories, we approach the future with confidence and hope.

We must lean into believing that He will make all things beautiful in their time. Specific times are for specific things. We have times for grief, for falling in love, for joy, for confiding fears, for being courageous, and all the rest of the human experience. Do you know what time you're in? Can you tell when it started and sense when it's ending? As we become aware of the stages of our lives, we see with new clarity. We can be intentional and free to choose how to move forward. We are deliberate to make the most of the stage we are in. We are free to enjoy it without the pressure of doing other things.

I don't want to live under the weight of expectations when I could live in the freedom of obedience. The boundaries of what we are called to do in a specific time allow us to wander freely within those limitations. We don't have to worry about what to do and what not to do. We seek out the purpose of the moment we are in and devote ourselves to pursuing joy in that thing we have chosen to do. Gone is the pressure of performing, achieving, and impressing. Instead, we stand taller and stronger just living. If you want a key to life, embrace God where you are now and let everything else break away.

LESSON 4

My mom took me to get my permit when I turned fifteen. We drove into town so I could take the exam at the DDS. After I passed, my mom handed the keys over and let me drive home. I hopped in the driver's seat and started my first real drive. I had spent years driving golf carts and occasionally sat behind the wheel when driving on our farm. This time, real cars with real strangers navigated all around me.

On our way home, we passed a Dairy Queen. That seemed like the perfect spot to celebrate. My little brother had tagged along for the ride that day, so my mom treated us both. I asked my mom to drive the rest of the way home so I could enjoy my sundae. She and I swapped seats, and we headed back to the farm.

About halfway back home, we stopped on a small country road behind a car waiting to turn left. I had turned in my seat to talk to my brother behind me. Both of us were still enjoying our treats. Suddenly, the back windshield of our van crashed under the force of the car behind us. I could see the terror on my brother's face and feel my mom reach her arm across me, doing all she could to keep us safe. Crushing metal screamed from behind us. Our van scraped the car turning left in front of us, but we avoided oncoming traffic and the steep shoulder to our right.

When all the cars stopped, we could see everyone was okay. Our van was totaled, but the worst we felt was post-accident shakiness and soreness. After insurance and contact information swapping, a relative drove us home.

I was far from eager to drive ever again. I had no desire to be in charge in a situation like that. I wished I had never gotten my permit. The sound of the accident echoed in my thoughts as I tried to fall asleep. My mom pushed me for months to drive more. Reluctantly, I signed up for driver's ed. Compilations of actual and fictitious car accident videos comprised most of the content. This didn't motivate me to drive safer; it solidified my fear that I should never drive again.

Practically, never driving again presented complications. I needed to get to school, and my dad's house, see friends, and take my siblings places. The option of not driving became less and less viable. Socially, not driving seemed like shooting myself in the foot. Being homeschooled is pretty lame in high school. Waiting for someone to pick me up and drop me off would not increase my social status. Cautiously, I took my driving test. Even with my lacking parallel parking skills, I got my license.

Over a decade later, the memory of that accident popped up in my mind. I began prayerfully journaling this memory. God, why is this coming up now? Is there something you're trying to say to me through it? The sound of the crash and my brother's scream passed through my mind. The comfort of my mom's arm reaching over to me followed. I wrote thoughts down as quickly as they came to record what God wanted to teach me through it.

We go about life, and bad things happen outside our control. People take, people leave, people die. We can talk about pain generally, but all of us see the faces of the ones who hurt us. We carry the sounds of windshields shattering and work through fears of driving again. We can't make sense of others' selfish decisions or why we had to be collateral damage of carelessness. We think of how different life could have been if we never got in the car, if the Dairy Queen order had taken two minutes longer to make, or if we had taken the long way home.

I still struggle to find purpose in my pain. I hear it's healthy to understand the role of pain in our lives, but I'd sooner go without it. I want to be blissfully ignorant, comfortably unaware, and unrealistically safe. That kind of ignorance, however, comes at a cost. Our choices and development are limited by such a high degree of security. Our relationships change when we don't allow anyone or anything close enough to hurt us. Still, we never fail to cause pain to one another eventually.

Lately, I've been able to make peace with not understanding the purpose of pain. I hope to learn more as I get older. So far, I've come to one important truth as my foundation. God is good, and that's enough for me to know right now.

We go places with God like I had gone to the DMV with my family. He enables us to achieve and accomplish amazing things for ourselves and others, just like they helped me get my permit. He gives us good gifts and takes the lead when we want to sit back and enjoy time with Him. He ensures our safety when the inconsideration or recklessness of those around us catastrophically impacts our lives. He is with us when we get hurt. He handles the legality of injustice and restoration. He is with us as we recover. He challenges us to get up again when we've been knocked down. That's the nature of God that my mom demonstrated the day I got my permit.

My mom probably could have told me we were about to be in an accident. She had a pretty good idea of how she would react to the car to cause minimal damage. With a car stopped in front of us, oncoming traffic to our left, a shoulder to our right, and the responsible car rolling sixty miles an hour up behind our stopped car, the collision could have been much worse. I've never felt angry with her for not warning us about the impending crash. Despite the damage, she took care of us with everything she had.

I have been angry with God when life crashes down. As a praying woman, I feel entitled to know when something terrible is about to happen. I feel bait-and-switched when I follow Him and end up in a rough situation. How could He let that happen? With all respect for those raw, honest questions that need to be asked, seeing the sovereignty of God now helps me understand how wrong I was to assume the worst of Him. Just like Job also realized, who are we to judge God?

The original sin, eating the fruit from the tree of the knowledge of good and evil, remains the propensity of our human nature. Given the right circumstances, reality distorts, and I see myself as someone worthy to judge. I decide what is good and what is evil. I decide who is good and who is evil. I know good from evil. I'm the authority on all things good and evil. That's an arrogant position when the Creator of the universe is in the same space.

Expressing my raw feelings before God is good, but judging God for what He does and doesn't do is not right. His perspective encompasses more than mine, and His existence is far beyond mine. I can't assume my twenty-something years of life could provide more wisdom and insight than His eternal presence. So, what can we do with the knowledge of good and evil?

We put down the fruit from that tree and strengthen ourselves with the fruit of the Spirit. The Spirit of God sustains us with love, joy, peace, longsuffering, kindness, goodness, gentleness, faithfulness, and self-control. We surrender to His supremacy when we step off the throne of judgment and invite God to determine the good and evil in our experiences. Our accusations toward Him and the world are exchanged for the fruit of His Spirit. Instead of screaming out our pain as we storm away from Him, we bring our hurt to Him because we can trust Him to heal us.

Imagine how real, tender, intimate love alters the experience of pain. Think of how peace and gentleness mend brokenness or how self-control and kindness can end cycles of damage. Picture goodness blossoming in deserts of disappointment and joy approaching like the dawn. How comforting is the faithfulness being made in you so you never have to fear what the future may hold? What a gift longsuffering is to those who live by the Spirit.

What if we held it before God and truly suffered through it instead of hiding or pushing away our pain? No shortcuts, numbing, dismissing, maybe not even deliverance from it. What if we trusted God as our Healer, Protector, Provider, Redeemer, and Savior? To patiently endure is to hold off our judgments of God's character until we see the completion of the work He has intended through our suffering.

I've felt desperate for God to intervene in my circumstances and frustrated by the time between devastation and deliverance. Circumstances contribute to my life, but they are not my life. Jesus is my life, and I come to the Father through Him. So even if my circumstances are in desperate need of miracles, I am held in the love of the Father with the life of Christ.

We have the choice to look at our circumstances and judge God through the refractions of Him in it all, or we can look at God and hold the pain of our circumstances before Him. We allow the work of the Spirit to produce longsuffering and whatever else He wants in us. We trust He will sustain us with something better than our judgments. We end every circumstance with a deeper and more intimate relationship with God.

This kind of living requires humility and surrender, which naturally follow an accurate understanding of who God is. But often, seeing God through our pain distorts our perception. Humility and surrender can also both naturally follow experiences with God's love. We find this in prayer. Ask God to show you His love amidst pain.

For a while, I had been waking up in the middle of the night with racing thoughts about an upcoming surgery. One tired morning, I drove to work and asked God to show me His love for me in some small way. I greeted a woman walking into the sanctuary right before our service started. She asked how I was doing, and I told her I was doing well overall but concerned about this procedure. It turns out she had surgery for the same issue years ago. Not only did this settle my heart about the surgery, but it also settled my heart before God. My spirit could rest knowing that God hears my prayers and loves me.

I have to get alone and ask God what He wants to say about my pain. "God, this hurts. What do You want to tell me right now? God, I'm uncomfortable. Who are You to me right now? God, I don't understand what You're doing. What do You say about this? God, I'm mad You haven't intervened like I want. Where are You right now?" Then I wait until I sense His response. Sometimes, it's like a thought crossing my mind that feels peaceful. Sometimes, it's a feeling of relief from my sadness. Sometimes, it's a random text of encouragement from a friend. Sometimes, it's the idea to do something specific, like make a cup of tea or have a meaningful conversation with someone.

The promise for us is to sow in tears and reap in joy. I don't want to waste my seeds of sadness, pain, and loss, scattering them to the wind when God promised an abundant harvest. I want to bury them in the soil of His love and tend the garden until I see His word fulfilled. I have to trust that He is Lord and He is Love. That's who He says He is.

LESSON 5

I grew up in the Bible Belt of the States. Some of my earliest memories were learning Bible stories and memorizing Scripture verses. The older I got, the more I discovered how difficult it is for some people to find access to a Bible. My first mission trip back in middle school was to a country where most villages only had one Bible they all shared. The Bible has yet to be translated into around 2,500 languages. That's 2,500 people-groups who cannot hear the Bible in their language of origin.

I wonder how different my faith would be if I didn't have the Bible and decades of teachers simplifying it for me. Taking the Bible for granted in my culture and context is far too easy. I have Bibles on my phone, laptop, nightstand in my room, shelves in my church, and parts of it now hidden in my heart. I have access to commentaries, scholars, preachers, teachers, and hundreds of believers further along in life than I am. My faith is deeply intertwined with the written Word. It's hard to imagine a time when people believed in God before the Bible was canonized. I am incredibly grateful for my access to the Bible. Before I tell you why, let's take a quick detour to talk about a Bible-less culture.

On a mission trip to Scotland, our team took a historical tour of the Celtic saints through the Highlands with one of our missionaries. He brought us to a stone circle where we learned about the Pictish people. The Picts were not well understood. They rivaled the Romans violently and eventually united under a king. We do know their stone circles were incredibly sacred sites.

Our missionary taught us that the Picts were a pagan group that worshiped nature. They worshiped the sun, the trees, the wind, the tides. I understand how they could fall into false worship. From their view, nature provided for them. They worshiped all its elements in return.

Celtic saints came to minister to this people group. The Picts did not have a written language. Rather than teaching the meaningful traditions and stories of the Roman faith, the saints taught them about God in a way that was meaningful to them. Seeing their reverence for the trees, the Pictish people were told how God created the trees. They were told that God is the Maker of the heavens. The saints didn't discredit what the Picts knew and believed; they taught them that God is more powerful and worthy of worship than anything in His marvelous creation. This truth is fundamental to Christianity: God is worthy. We see His glory reflected in the world around us. The revelation of His goodness is not limited to the pages of the Bible.

When I was young, my family occasionally practiced "creation meditation" based loosely on Romans 1:19-20. We picked something in nature and sat with it for a time, pondering what about this creation revealed God. How do the veins running through a leaf point to God's delicate and intentional design? How does the sun reflect God's sustenance of our lives through light? How does the stilling effect of quiet waters reveal the Spirit hovering over the depths of our hearts?

I fell out of practicing Creation Meditation sometime in adulthood but recently reincorporated it into my spiritual disciplines. I feel the pull to nature, especially after weeks in the city, and wonder if God is drawing me back to the earth to meet with me. We can find reasons to worship and commit ourselves to God outside of Scripture. We can integrate our knowledge of the God of the Bible into everything we see. That being said, it's harder to gauge truth without Scripture. This is one of the reasons the Bible is such a gift to me. I am immensely grateful to live in a time where the Bible is accessible.

The Bible helps us discern what is true and what is deceitful. Lies may grow in our belief system while we are in the world. Many of these lies can be combated with the Holy Spirit when we recall the truth in Scripture. If I begin to believe I am unloved, I can ask the Holy Spirit how John 3:16 applies to me. If I lose a sense of peace, I can ask the Spirit what John 14:27 means. If I hear that all roads lead to God, I can ask the Spirit how to interpret John 14:6. So many words and beliefs that hurt us or do not sit well in our Spirit can be corrected gently by Scripture.

I have been reading this collection of wisdom and testimonies my whole life. I am still learning. I still see God in new yet familiar ways through passages I have known for decades. I am still unearthing questions I have never asked before leading to answers I never considered. The Bible is a gift for our minds and spirits in this lifetime.

Early in the Gospels, we see Satan attempting to tempt Jesus by twisting words of Scripture. Jesus was not fooled. He did not just know the words of Scripture to recite; He knew the Author. Understanding the Bible apart from knowing the Author is insufficient to sustain faith. It's also not the point of faith in the first place. The Bible connects us to God by revealing His character, teaching truth from Him, and instructing us on how to be with Him.

Many of my friends have experienced the Bible being used out of context or outside the boundaries of godly love. I can't imagine Jesus' dying wish would be that Christians in the 21st century would use His words to push people away from Him. Our zeal for righteousness can burn people if we aren't careful. I do not support tolerant, watered-down Christianity. I am advocating for truth in love, discipleship long-term, patience in affliction, and laying down our self-righteousness to share in Christ's righteousness. Have righteous anger and uncompromising truth, but don't twist His words to hurt the ones He wants to heal. This call goes for sinners and saints, pulpit and pew, left and right, love one another. *Love* one another.

I do not believe the Bible is best studied alone; to get the full effect of the Scriptures, we need to read it with the Holy Spirit. He guides us into all truth according to Jesus. He leads us deeper into the heart of God through Scripture rather than us simply retaining more Scripture as we read through it. Eternal life isn't memorizing Scripture (although that is a helpful tool); eternal life is knowing the Father. We don't need Him to *know* what was said but to *understand* what was said and transform because of it. With the Holy Spirit, we have a miraculous opportunity to learn the Bible this way.

A common use of the Bible is for edification and instruction in group settings. Sermons revolve around passages of Scripture. Devotionals explore parts of Scripture. Commentaries explain sections of Scripture. Small groups or discipleship groups study through the Bible or these secondary and tertiary sources of the Bible. I find comfort that the words in the Book on my bedside table are the same ones sustaining the missionaries I know, the imprisoned believers in conflict-ridden places, and many who are at their life's end.

I lay my fuzzy floor pillow next to the coffee table in the living room and light a candle to read this Book while someone on the other side of the world recites it on the edge of a mountain as they pray over their city. I share a story from the Gospel with a Muslim woman I met on the street while someone in a hospital prays Scriptures over their sick child. I sing the same Psalm in the church that another woman shares with her church as she dedicates her son to the Lord. This Book isn't just a classic or popular read. The Bible is a gift, sustaining the hope of God's people wherever they can access it.

This has been the case for generations. I find courage and stamina from reading the Scriptures, remembering all the saints who have gone before me. This thread of faith is longer than the lineage I can see. It runs through time. Throughout centuries, believers have been learning from the Holy Spirit as they pour over Scriptures in prayer and study. Brilliant theologians have made mysteries plain to us in their dedication to the Bible. Renowned evangelists have brought millions to the Lord using the same verses I occasionally use as wallpaper on my phone. People engaged with God through the Bible long before you or I ever lived.

Many heroes of the faith had pieces of our Scripture committed to their memories and shared during their gatherings. I am inspired by wondering how many believers have had the Lord's prayer pass through their lips since those famous words were first uttered on the mountain, as we see in Matthew 6. How many people has that prayer touched? How many situations has it been prayed over? How many encounters with God have people had over the centuries? The legacy of faith is so much bigger than just me. The faithfulness of God to His creation began long before my life did.

I do not want to take the Bible for granted. I want to know God better because of it. I also don't want to limit my understanding of God strictly to the pages of Scripture. I hope the Bible informs my understanding of God in the world around me. He created everything we see. The earth reflects His majesty in fragments all around us. I dream of seeing the world transformed by the Author and Perfector of our faith. The Ancient Texts remind us of this: He loves us. Don't forget. He *loves* us.

LESSON 6

I generally alternate between books in three categories: science fiction, psychology, and physics. I finished a streak of social psychology books and decided to focus on *A Brief History of Time* before returning to *The 48 Laws of Power*. As I read about the misconception of absolute rest, I thought about the popular psychology circulating through my social environment on rest. I'm a strong advocate for good sleep and relaxation. Rest is necessary, but sometimes we can crave and idealize downtime so much that it steals away from our living and overall functioning. Rest is essential, but it must be an integration of our lives rather than an escape from them.

Like the early fathers of physics, we need to change our idea of rest. Rather than rest being the natural state we occasionally move from, rest is what we do, along with all the other things we do. The first Law of Motion is that things at rest tend to stay at rest. A friend of mine would say a theory about productivity that is similar. When we're in motion, we remain in motion. If our long-term priority is rest, we will become lazy and exhausted. If our long-term priority is getting things done, we will be bustling with things to do.

As humans, our goal should be the integration of motion and rest. How can we exert ourselves fully during the day to rest fully during the night? This integration is how we become more balanced, have higher capacity, are efficient, and are better sustained over long periods. Rest is about restoring what has been depleted and celebrating what is complete. When it becomes more than that, it morphs into escapism and lethargy. Those cause us to disconnect from our people, aspirations, and sense of purpose. The best way to experience rest is in its proper portion.

Motion is about experiencing life. We want to make the most of every day because that will bring us the most fulfillment. The practical application is not busyness but purpose. What is the purpose of your day? How can you pursue it? Most of us have jobs. We have to work to pay the bills. Hopefully, we get jobs we enjoy and can contribute to society how we want to. That's not always the case. So, while our 9-5 may not drive us out of bed and into the office daily, other related goals might. I want to make friends at work. I want to provide for my family. I want to save for a vacation. I want to obtain a promotion. I want to remind the world that people are kind. I want to share my knowledge. The more of these goals we can create for ourselves, the fuller our days will be. Then, work is less about mundane tasks and more about cultivating your life.

I helped my sister, Sarah, move across the country with her husband and one-year-old. On our way to the airport, we discussed goals and purpose. Her ten-year goals were easy to accomplish from 16-26. She knew she wanted to go to college, get a job she liked, and start a family. Ten-year goals became more complex after that. She has her husband's and daughter's lives to consider in every aspect of her planning. There are exponentially more outcomes to each decision and more factors in play as they build their lives together. One of the most beautiful things Sarah told me was that her daughter, Clara, feeds off her emotions. When Sarah is happy, Clara is happy. When Sarah is stressed, Clara is stressed. In this stage of life, she found purpose in settling in their new home and investing in new relationships. The more she enjoyed her new environment, the more her daughter would feel pleasant emotions and a connection to her. That's a sense of purpose she can hold onto through a massive transition.

Our intentions matter as we integrate rest and motion. Making busywork for ourselves does no favors for us. Preoccupation with rest will get us in the habit of thinking we don't have enough to make it through the day. Life is not scarce when we have a purpose. Our lives become fuller when passion, commitment, intimacy, and love drive us.

Prayer focuses me on my purpose. When I wake up in a funk or not entirely rested, I can ask God to bless my day and spend it looking for those blessings. On the way to work, I often ask God what He wants me to accomplish that day. Most times, it's simply to love the people before me. When I'm worn out in the evenings and just want to get in bed, I ask God to be near me in whatever activity would bring me a bit of fun or contentment with life. If I can't sleep, I'll talk to God about my day and what I found meaningful.

You can roll through life without optimism. Plenty of people live and die average lives. If you want more out of life, you have to put more into your life. Cultivate ambition. Protect your sense of purpose. Choose to live well and choose to rest in service of that. This is the power of intention.

It is a choice to believe that life is worth living, that life can be purposeful, that purpose has meaning, that meaning requires intentionality, and that intentions have power. Those choices can be challenging. Each choice we make in that direction is a step closer to the kind of life we would dream of if we were unafraid to be disappointed or hurt.

Occupationally and academically, intentionality looks like high achievement through discipline. Discipline is necessary for the pursuit of our goals. It dwindles without intentionality and is required to build intentionality. They are intertwined. Discipline is a hard habit to form in our character but reaps the best fruit when mixed with purpose.

My friends say they appreciate that I'm intentional in our friendships. They know they are one of the highest priorities in my life. If I say I will pray for them, I will tell them what I'm praying for. If I feel disconnected from them, I'm going to reach out. If I commit to something with them, I will follow through.

Relationally, intentionality looks like loyalty and strong relationships. It's dependability and commitment. It's thoughtfulness and consideration. Our relationships require a degree of intentionality ever to exist. The more we invest, the more we gain.

I love my life. I love my work, my family, my friends, my hobbies, my home, and my prospects for the future. Five years ago, I didn't. Life felt like a big blob of disconnected things. I didn't know what was happening or what to do about it. I've been chipping away at the formless chunk of marble that was my life to create what I have now. It required a lot of prayer, a lot of direction, a lot of help, a lot of perspective shifts, and a lot of faithfulness.

In life, intentionality looks like faithfulness. I want to be devoted to the work God is doing in me and creating around me. I want to be committed to the hope that my life can positively influence the world. I want to choose what's good for me rather than be enslaved to desires and cravings for the latest thing that appeals to me.

Intentionality benefits every aspect of our lives. It's the little steps that we take along the road of perseverance. We choose to move, rest, grow our capacity, influence society, strengthen our relationships, and enjoy life. Sometimes, those choices will be easy and natural. Sometimes, they'll be grueling and costly. But every time, the decision to be intentional will be worth it.

LESSON 7

In all the hustle and bustle of life, I sometimes forget how natural living and loving are. A couple of years ago, I couldn't imagine ever feeling as content and grateful as I do now. I thought I would have to be lying to say I appreciate life. Now, I wake up early, energized for the day instead of anxious or full of dread. I go to work with purpose and leave feeling accomplished. I hang out with friends and family, feeling relaxed and happy. I go to bed thankful and ready to see what the next day holds. It's funny how easily fooled we are by our emotions. When my circumstances were terrible, I thought my life was awful. Now that my circumstances are good, my life is good. As I mature spiritually, I hope to put more weight on the Word of God and less on the fragments of the world I see.

This part of my life feels like a brief montage in a movie with cheery music before something life-altering in the worst way happens. I know that's my fear of the future, trying to keep its place in the home of my heart. I also know it's not entirely untrue. This stage of my life will inevitably end. My life won't be smooth sailing for years to come; that's unrealistic. But let's look at a few things we can learn from easy times.

Ease is for enjoyment. Low pressure or low responsibility gives us a higher capacity to pursue joy. I want to make the most of times when little is required of me, and a lot is available to me. My mom is one of my favorite friends with whom I enjoy easy days. For months, my mom and I went back and forth planning and replanning a trip together. She had a full plate. I was kicking off my career with a new job. Slipping away on vacation kept slipping further away from us. Finally, we found a weekend. We headed to sunny Florida with no responsibilities, agenda, or pressure– only hopes of what could be. My mom and I could talk about anything for hours on end. That weekend, we did. We threw out ideas of the top fun things on our fun lists and knocked them off individually. The weekend was perfect. We ate the best cookie I've ever had. We walked over twenty miles in seventy-degree weather and watched fireworks in the evening. We screamed and laughed like children on our favorite rides.

We hadn't accomplished anything of significance. We didn't create much change or have much of an impact on the world around us. But I'll keep that memory with me as long as I can. When times get less manageable, I'll know the joy I felt was real, so it's a possibility again. Easy times are a gift. They can be incredibly rare. We can't predict how long they might last. Enjoying them is the best thing we can do with them because recalling them later will give us hope when we need it the most.

Easy times keep molehills as molehills. Making mountains out of molehills is more likely to happen when stress piles up. I had a substantial meltdown in the fall, right after I had dropped out of graduate school. Stress was high, and I was losing another grandpa to another terrible disease. The interview process for my desired job was much longer than I anticipated. The bills were sucking the progress out of my savings account. I had a health concern that I knew needed medical attention, but I was too scared to open that can of worms.

I surveyed my situation and decided that making a doctor's appointment was one thing I could control. I hyped myself up and booked an appointment with a doctor in my area as soon as possible. My appointment disappointed me. I didn't feel heard by the doctor and left feeling more afraid. She recommended several invasive tests that scared me, too. I felt so much overwhelming anxiety after the appointment that I had to pull my car into a parking lot to compose myself before driving again. The anxiety grew into a fog of uncertainty over the next couple of days, culminating in a storm of emotion. In my big meltdown of spiraling thoughts, uncontrollable tears, and pounding heartbeats, I felt paralyzed with fear. The fear response I had didn't match the situation. But watching someone close to you dying can be a scary thing, which didn't pair well with my pre-existing medical phobia. Not knowing when you'll have an income or insurance again is not the best foundation to stand on when the doctor orders further testing.

During that period, my grandpa passed away. The kin who attended his memorial and celebration of life repeatedly remarked how he sought out and enjoyed the beauty in the world. My grandma helped me make sense of death and loss through her wisdom and example. I got the job I wanted with a livable income to pay my bills and insurance. Life naturally evolved into a simpler, livelier time. The stressors slowed down, and my enjoyment of life increased exponentially. The only residue from that chapter was my health concern.

I had time to approach my concern well this time. I talked to my therapist about my irrational fear and asked friends to pray for me. I got recommendations from people I trusted for potential doctors. I made an appointment with a doctor who cared for me, communicated a strategy moving forward, and encouraged me to call if I had concerns between appointments. I trusted her enough to complete the first test round that day. I'm equally proud and embarrassed to say that it was the first time I had lab work done that I didn't hysterically cry or pass out. Full disclosure, I felt so nervous I couldn't hear the lab tech talking to me. I saw her mouth moving, but my brain heard distant mumbles. Still, I faced my fear and lived through it. I want to take advantage of the courage, support, and strategies easy times offer to face fears and conquer giants in my life. I want to embrace them with immense thankfulness and respond with compassion for others.

Easy times for me don't mean easy times for everyone. When I'm enduring difficulties, I want to be cared for by people who aren't overwhelmed by their situations. Once that weight lifts, I want to be the one to help people in the same way.

Persevering when life is easy doesn't take grit. It feels so good that it doesn't even feel like perseverance, just living. Excitement for life catapults you into the next moment. Contentment with circumstances charms you with wonder for tomorrow. Enjoying the present satiates the thirst for answers to life's big questions. This fleeting, romantic, carefree experience is a gift. Although easy times may correlate with money and resources, their essence is peace and belonging. The richest and poorest men in the world may be burnt out at work with emotional turmoil in the home. Both could happen upon or achieve moments engulfed in beauty, and all is right in their small worlds for a time.

One of the things I love most about Jesus is that He gives me peace and a sense of belonging. He trades my weariness for His ease. I enjoy time with Him. He's the hopeful, reassuring voice that promises moments surrounded by beauty.

When my life is easy, I want to be with Him. He's fun and kind. It's silly but a staple of my relationship with Him. He's everywhere I go, filling my life with joy. He's my everything. I don't want easy times if He's not in them. He's why I feel at ease, whether difficult or easy. I'm okay whether having a meltdown on a small couch in a dark room or eating German gingerbread cookies with freshly made caramel and cream cheese icing. No matter what happens, it's me and Him. I wouldn't trade that kind of security for anything.

With that kind of love as a foundation, loving others is easy. Sharing good feelings is natural and fun, contagious even. The interactions and exchanges with people around us feel better when we abide by the love of Jesus.

My job involves being in the community weekly, talking to people about their needs. Compassion is inevitable when you see the conditions some people live in and the lack they live with. I feel a stronger desire to serve now that I've played with the kids whose parents can hardly pay the bills and met the girls rescued from sex trafficking. The pull to love people is compelling. At some point, we must prioritize being the ease in other people's lives. When we have some capacity to give more, give more. When we don't, rearrange to get it.

Changing our minds to be more generous, kind, and loving is the fruit of being grounded in our communities. As we get to know the people in our lives and build relationships with strangers near us, our perspectives broaden, and our empathy grows. We don't have to assign ourselves acts of kindness; we can simply be kind.

I don't want to waste my time of ease with selfish ambition. I want to relieve those who are weighed down and limping along. As I persevere, I want to help as many people along the way as I can.

LESSON 8

I don't remember when my anxiety first started. I remember appointments with neurologists and psychologists as a child, figuring out ways to manage the tremor in my hands. I try to forget the countless nights I sensed a looming presence watching me as I lay awake. I'm all too familiar with the cloud that suddenly takes over my mind; no single thought is clear or notably louder than the rest. Dizziness overwhelms my composure; I feel so far from my body that it's like I'm watching myself cry on the floor.

My parents and older sister knew how to make me feel safe and cared for. Their support, prayers, and wisdom provided the security I couldn't find within my skin. Every heartache and misfortune that came my way trapped me in a dark cage of self-preservation as my mind dramatized my already fearful view of the world. The older I got, the more embarrassed I felt to ask for help.

Sometime in high school, I started experiencing what I call "funks." Seemingly, out of nowhere, I lose motivation and enjoyment of things that I usually love. A counselor explained that I am a deep feeler and I have big emotions. The influence of these big emotions on my appetite, exercise, social life, and spirituality is exhausting.

With the support of my social network, I have become confident in adequately functioning through these acute anxious episodes and depressive funks. As unwanted as these are, they are not unbearable. I know the love of my God, family, and friends will carry me over troubled waters. I'm blessed to have a circle that welcomes carrying one another's burdens when the load is too heavy. I've spent years curating this solidarity in my social life. It has been the sweetest work to rest in now.

A handful of times this year, I had mind-numbing, chest-crushing, tear-drenched moments, and I wasn't alone for a single one of them. Even if it came on when I was by myself, someone was holding me or praying over me by the end of it. I had no idea how powerful trusting good people with my insecurities could be. Their love has been big enough to curb even my most prominent emotions.

Love can conquer anything. My friends' fierce love has protected me from realistic and unrealistic fears. Their quiet love has crept through the lethargy of my mornings spent too long in bed. Loneliness exponentially compounds our experiences of pain, but love reframes those experiences to bring peace.

Opening up to safe people can restore parts of us. Picture your soul as a house. Damages incur over time. If left untended, time will require a remodel. You may be able to do a lot of the renovation alone. Eventually, you'll need other qualified people to help. Usually, having good friends to help makes the process more bearable. Some things would be possible alone but easier with others. And some things would just be more enjoyable with others. The same goes for our inner processes of restoration.

We have secret ideas of self-actualization, but we are so insecure about showing people our mess that we don't progress much toward our highest potential. We get tired. We give up. We need people in our lives who will catch onto the vision we have for ourselves and leave judgment at the door. Part of this requires investing in relationships with good people. Another part requires cultivating friendships that uphold values of honest communication and mutual respect. My friends and I tell each other what we believe in, want for ourselves, and hope for each other. Then, we hold each other to those with a bit of space for adaptability. It's incredible. My community is one of the things I am most proud of and grateful for.

Once we've found people we want to try being honest with, we must let them in. We must initiate the cycle of asking for help and showing up for each other. Why? Because it's mutually beneficial. It's a gift you can contribute to every meaningful friendship, simply requiring that you extend trust to someone who has done nothing yet to break it. You can rely on people and let them depend on you in return.

As wonderful as interdependence with good people can be, relying on people too strongly leads you into codependency. This doesn't necessarily mean we should pull back from people, but simply step up a little more ourselves.

A few times throughout my life, I've felt so terrified at night I didn't want to sleep alone. When I opened up to the people closest to me each time, they said the same thing. "Try." They were challenging and encouraging me to be independent. They knew I was safe. I needed to believe I was safe, too. Irrational fear distorted my sense of reality. Neutral ground is hard to find mentally in such a fearful state, so I knew I had two options. I could give into the fear and play out fantasies of my worst nightmares until morning, or I could try to push back against the fear.

I struggled both of those nights as I fought for relief. But now those struggles are "Ebenezers" of my fight for my freedom. Years have flown by since the last time I felt so afraid. I can see how God stirred up hope that my nights wouldn't be panicked or paranoid. I can see how He created a new reality for me from that hope.

Awareness of our internal world is necessary for growth. But awareness alone is not enough. Awareness can lead us from ignorance or shame to self-acceptance and love, but that's as far as it will take us. We have to pair our awareness with the expectation and desire for something better, or else we are selling ourselves short. We won't reach self-actualization from our secret dreams for ourselves until we partner with the belief that we can change.

Hope compels us beyond impossible obstacles to reach our highest potential. Our fears and struggles can't hang on that long; they can't outlast hope, especially hope rooted in Jesus Christ. Jesus is the One who empowers us and sustains us as we overcome through His victory. When He died on the Cross, resurrected, ascended to heaven, and sent us His Spirit to dwell within us, He created the opportunity for us to have a never-ending and whole life. He exchanges our ashes for beauty and mourning for joy. He has always been rescuing us, but God incarnate revealed a closeness to Divinity that the world hadn't seen since the Garden of Eden.

With the power of the Spirit in us, that same Spirit that raised Christ from the dead, we can tear down obstacle after obstacle. Our habits and brokenness are old ways shed as we grow in the likeness of our eternal Conqueror. Hope in Christ is the confidence that we are not stuck in a pit. Hope is when we scare away our fears and failures with the death and resurrection of Jesus. We can wedge the Cross between us and our fears or funks until the bond breaks.

When we believe that restoration is available and accessible, nothing can stop us. Hope sustains our fights. Doubt and exhaustion will push us around as we press on, but the people around us can help. Great friendships will remind us of hope and show us the pathways we see to walk in greater hope for ourselves.

The truth of the matter is that you are worth loving. You are worth fighting for. God declared it. He loves you and fights for you. Hopefully, you have people in your life who love you and fight for you. You can love and fight for yourself. Steering clear of narcissism and aggression, you can rest in an awareness that you are an incredible creation and a hope that you are on your way to complete restoration.

I am a huge fan of my friends and family loving on me. But their affection will never replace the contentment I feel between God and me. I know, without a shadow of a doubt, He loves me. His love toward me looks like comfort and favor among thousands of other qualities I've yet to discover. Even in my shakiest moments of anxiety and longest funks, I feel the undercurrent of God's passion for me. His love is the foundation of truth that does not crack or crumble.

I'm also a huge fan of my friends and family fighting for me. Being cared for, provided for, and protected feels so good. I'm incredibly grateful for how my friends worked on my behalf in good and bad times just so my life might be a little better. But their efforts combined could never compare to the advocacy of Jesus on my behalf. He who lives to intercede for me has also given everything to defeat the only thing separating Him from me. When I'm ready to throw in the towel, I know He's not. He won't. He created me with the love of a Father, nurtured me through intimacy, and molded me through friendship. He values me and desires me. If He says I'm worth rescuing, redeeming, and restoring, I believe Him.

The choice to open up to people is risky and sometimes scary. Pursuing what God purchased for me is ominous and occasionally frustrating. But in these choices, we have access to more hope than despair. Giving up steals my motivation, enjoyment, appetite, vibrancy, relationships, and who knows what else. On the other hand, sharing the load with the people around me leads to encouragement, connection, stronger relationships, and eventual victory. I can fight for hope, my life, and my love. So can you. Whether you have an army, a friend, or stand alone, God is fighting for you. He loves you.

LESSON 9

Alissa became one of my first friends when I moved to Atlanta. I had just arrived in this huge, unfamiliar city. All I knew to do was find a church. That's where I found Alissa. She and her husband Matt figuratively and literally created space for me to feel like I belonged at church and in this new city. They welcomed me, hung out with me, finagled me into a job at the church, and shuffled offices around so I could work closer to everyone. I am so thankful for them.

Alissa is the most summer girl I've ever met. She loves the sunshine and loves to be tan. Alissa turns into a Greek goddess just looking at the sun which is quite the contrast to my fair and freckled skin that boils in the sun. We wanted to make the most out of a beautiful, bright day so we picked a hiking trail up in the mountains.

We headed to Toccoa, Georgia, with blue Powerade and peanut butter crackers. Alissa is great at having fun and having deep-heart conversations. Our drive up was a mixture of goofing off and deeper conversations. Time flew, and we found ourselves at the trailhead of Panther Creek Falls. "Temporarily closed" marked the entrance to the trail in an unavoidable way. The closest trail was forty-five minutes away but had a waterfall. So we sulked back to the car and headed off to Raven Cliff Falls.

Raven Cliff Falls started rough. We couldn't find the trailhead. We cluelessly trekked past some older men at a picnic table a few times and tried following a young couple. They didn't know where to go either. Finally, we found a helpful woman who directed us down the path, across the street, and over a small bridge where the trail began.

We crossed a stream on a pile of old tree trunks and walked near the river the whole trail. Tall trees covered us with shade, and the breeze kept us from sweating too much. Raven Cliff lacked Panther Creek's intensity, but I loved the relaxed feel. The trail is less than four miles, so I didn't feel too worn out by the end. We climbed up on a rock when we reached the waterfall to pause. Walking outside and talking is one of my favorite pastimes. Sitting by a waterfall and talking is even better. My soul is quick to find rest by water. I had not realized how much I needed it.

The hike wasn't all beautiful. I saw a snake coiled up on a rock, which threatened to ruin my whole experience, but I managed to let that go. We both slipped and tripped our fair shares on the way to the waterfall. The good moments upstaged the bad. We greeted many strangers in passing and befriended a travel nurse near the biggest waterfall.

The walk back to the car flew by. We made fewer mistakes stepping in mud puddles than on the way to the waterfall, and both worked up an appetite. We rested at a sandwich shop by the river in downtown Helen and then returned home.

Paul the Apostle instructed the Church to continue in the grace of God. With hiking fresh on my mind, I wondered if grace is better understood as where we walk rather than what we walk toward. I used to think that grace came after. Grace is what meets us at our lowest and lifts us. Grace is what covers our sins after we repent. Grace is the intervention or moment with God we need when we need it. Thinking grace is like the waterfall at the end of a trail is somewhat true. But if we stop there, we might believe that grace is something we earn.

The simplest definition of grace to me is the favor of God. Paul the Apostle says it's by grace we are saved, which is the gift of God. This grace, this gift of God that brings salvation, is a theme in Scripture. This salvation is the story of the Gospel: God so loved the world that He gave His Son to die for our sins so that we may spend eternity with Him. God looked at you and me and said, "Wow, I want them." The grace that saved us is God's favor toward us. He chose us. We are His favorites. Grace is not something to pursue and acquire; grace is God's gift to us to receive. The nature of grace is that it is freely extended to us by God's volition. He gave us salvation from bondage into the freedom of extravagant love.

My obscure fascination with (and limited understanding of) quantum physics inspired me with another idea of grace. I love learning about "spacetime." This conceptual fusion of space and time produces a four-dimensional visualization of events. Imagine you're in a giant box with TIME etched into the walls, ceilings, and floors. You can only walk in one direction, which is the present. You are moving away from the past and toward the future, but you cannot be anywhere except the present. Now you've grasped how the concept of spacetime applies to us, at least as much as I have.

The connection between space and time is inextricable. If I drive from my house to yours, time has elapsed, and space has been crossed. I can only go from my house to yours by spending time and crossing space.

What if grace, like the concept of spacetime, is not necessarily linear? What if grace is spatial as well? Instead of viewing grace like divine intervention post-sin, I could view grace as the space in which I live. I walk, breathe, decide, feel, love, and change in the grace of God. It is divine intervention, but not confined to a moment. Just as God is engaged in every moment without being trapped in any moment, His grace persists. God is not limited to time and space; He fills and overflows each moment with grace. His grace is sufficient; it is not going to run out. Grace surrounds us; it is the presence we reside in as we are sanctified. Grace is God with us.

The idea of indulging sin becomes much more repulsive when I think about being immersed in the grace of God. I don't want to make choices that blatantly oppose the One who has surrounded me in His favor. Even when the temptation is right before me, the grace around me is more extraordinary. Learning God's nearness and awareness of His grace is crucial to living well.

When the Spirit led Jesus into the wilderness, temptation was present. But He was immersed in the favor of God; He's the Father's Beloved. In the wilderness, He rejected temptation over and over. We are more prepared to choose righteousness when we acknowledge the favor of God. Wouldn't it be great to live in the strength of grace and reject temptation repeatedly? I want to surrender my understanding of grace as an antidote and submit to learning grace as the desire of God that envelops me. I want to walk confidently, knowing God wants me to live with Him now through eternity.

Jesus promised His disciples that the Holy Spirit would come to us who believed when He returned to the Father. When the Holy Spirit did in Acts 4, the grace was so strong in each of them that no one around was in need. The disciples, like you and I, could have devised an extensive inventory of what they needed moments before the Holy Spirit came. They had spiritual, emotional, physical, relational, and vocational needs. They didn't have to. Their only instruction was to go to Jerusalem and wait. But the Holy Spirit's nearness brought grace that met every need. I don't know how this is possible. I know that the encounters I have experienced with the closeness of God satisfied my needs in the moments they came; this is grace.

I cannot imagine a more peaceful world than a world of grace. We need a world of justice and wholeness, but I see in the New Testament the miraculous gift of God's grace at the heart of every good thing. His favor is extended to us. We simply choose it because He chose us first. The decision in front of you is to live in the truth of grace or to live in a lie that God is not with you, offering you the Gospel of salvation.

Every year, I pick out a theme for my birthday that will last until the following birthday. Whatever I choose is my goal, prayer focus, and the lens through which I view my circumstances. I started the habit after years of watching my mom do it. I chose "grace" as my birthday theme. Grace is my middle name. Maybe exploring grace for a year would inform my sense of self and purpose.

I told Alissa about my intentions to delve into the grace. Alissa bought me a gray pullover with "grow in grace" written in beautiful, white cursive across the front. I love to come home and curl up in my pullover when I'm journaling to God about all I'm learning and still want to learn. The way I am growing in grace now is by choosing to believe that grace surrounds me. This truth requires a perspective shift.

I had been surviving for months by trying to take life a day at a time. I didn't have the capacity to look further ahead. I had broken apart my life into many, many pieces. Halfway through my year on grace, I felt like God wanted to begin putting it all back together. I had no idea what that meant. Day by day, bit by bit, I learned how to trade in my fragmented outlook on life for an eternal perspective.

I paused to worship on a busy Monday afternoon. The song said that we become like Jesus as we behold Jesus. I realized I had been trying to "zoom out" enough on my life to grasp an eternal perspective. Unfortunately, I don't have an expansive enough view of time and space to see my life in the scope of eternity. I am incapable of seeing what I cannot see. Finally, I found the key to my perspective shift. It's Jesus. Of course, it is.

I can't tell you what Panther Creek Falls looks like because I've never seen it. But someone who has been to Panther Creek can tell me what it looks, sounds, feels, and smells like. I can't see my life, especially considering my eternal life in Christ. But I can talk to Jesus. From His perspective, He can teach and tell me what my life looks like.

I won't see the grace of God encompassing my life apart from God. He reveals it to me. God's grace for us has been and will be. If you need more grace, ask God to show you where it is.

His grace and His nearness are, in many ways, the same. We are not without. Our beliefs and perspectives can trip us up, but His grace saves us. Like my hike with Alissa, we'll slip up less the more we get to know the ground where we walk. Praise God, we walk in grace.

LESSON 10

Ashlyn and I met in a dance group on the University of Georgia's campus during my sophomore year. One of us hates dancing; neither of us dances well. I can only assume it was an act of God that brought us to that dance group. We both wanted friends but didn't immediately hit it off.

I interned with Ashlyn at a campus ministry two years later. We spent plenty of time in groups but weren't close friends for the entire first year. I wanted to be friends with her. She wore Doc Martens and Birkenstocks exclusively. She was much cooler than I was with her messy blonde bun, countless piercings, and stacked rings.

At the beginning of our second year, I texted her asking if she wanted to hang out. By the grace of God, she said yes, and I knew I had a shot at friendship. She also joined my small group that year. That's when the fun began.

Our small group wasn't like others. Our leader set up a city-wide scavenger hunt with a Polaroid camera for us to take pictures at each spot we stopped when she was out of town for one week. She built a vast and beautiful fort for us in her home for another meeting. We had a dinner of tomato soup with fancy grilled cheese, followed by a dance party and a great sleepover. She had handmade soft feather decorations for each of us as a parting gift. When we were going through hard times, small groups meant going to the store to pick out ice cream and eating in the comfort of her living room. Once every few months, we would have our famous nap small group. We'd turn on a movie and all rest for a solid, uninterrupted hour and a half. These community-building, sweet times cultivated the perfect environment for great friendships to form. We learned a lot about each other over that year.

Ashlyn is the girl who will say what everyone is thinking. She's one of those call-it-like-it-is people who doesn't let you get away with discrepancies between what you say and what you do. She's candid and loaded with questions. Nothing is off limits as she explores the minds, beliefs, and lifestyles of those she meets. As I mentioned before, she's cool. The way she dresses and talks makes my inner-homeschooled-child wish I could be like her.

The more I got to know Ashlyn, the better my life became. Our small group would order three jalapeno queso cups for each Mexican food night: one for me, one for Ashlyn, and one for the rest. As far as cheese dip is concerned, she's my kindred spirit. Her recipe for the best queso ever is pinned to the side of my refrigerator.

She and I could laugh for hours together. She stuck by me like a guard dog through some of the most challenging times I've seen, and I've gotten to sit with her through some of her most difficult moments, too. One of the most unique aspects of Ashlyn in my close circle is how much she believes in me.

Ashlyn calls me a unicorn. She makes a point of reminding me often that there's no one like me. I hope everyone can have a friend like her. It feels so good for someone to know the good, bad, and ugly about you and still say you're special.

Over the last few years, Ashlyn has been in my corner, believing in me for the big and small moments. She makes me want to live up to my potential and stay true to who I am. She prays for me, calls me out, and loves me into being better than I was yesterday. Without friendships like hers, we don't make it far in life. We need people to see the good parts of us and hold onto them when we lose sight of them. We need people who help us carry our burdens when they're heavy and people who tell us that we can make it through hard things.

It's not good for us to be alone. If I didn't have the friends I've had, I wouldn't be where I am in life now. I can think of plenty of mornings I wouldn't have gotten out of bed if my friends hadn't picked me up for coffee runs. Along with those are a string of bad decisions I might have made if I didn't tell my friends what I had in mind first. Friends act as guardrails for the paths in our lives. When I step back and look at my life, one of the things I am most thankful for is that God surrounds me with good people wherever I go.

We naturally become like the people we hang around. Parents or grandparents try to tell us this when we hang out with "the wrong crowd" in high school, and there's substantial truth to it. Intimate relationships are qualified by the ability to be vulnerable, even with the dark parts of yourself. You develop personal relationships with those you open yourself to and those who respond to you as well. You determine the level of intimacy you create with the people in your life, so choose wisely. Whether you acknowledge it or not, they're going to change you. But this isn't inherently a bad thing!

Healthy relationships are characterized by independent individuals who are attached. Our intimate relationships must balance self-expansion and self-preservation. Self-expansion is exploring what is important to the other person– valuing what they value. Self-preservation is maintaining your sense of self and the values you hold intrinsically. If you lose yourself in the other person, your relationship is no longer healthy. If you don't adapt to the person you're attached to, harmony is out of reach. If the other person loses their sense of identity in you, you're unhealthy again. Great relationships are carefully, respectfully, and intentionally made.

We must choose to be vulnerable with people, knowing they will change things about us. They're going to add values and perspectives to our experience of life. They will push and challenge us, colliding with us and knocking us into new trajectories. Who we trust with the deepest parts of ourselves is vitally important. Close relationships inherently make us worse, keep us stuck, or improve us.

My conviction is to live in peace with everyone. I want to be friendly and build relationships with whoever I cross paths with. Chatting with the grocery store clerk or striking up conversations at the dog park are worthwhile relationships. Those little interactions can hold tremendous power. People feel overlooked and undervalued everywhere. We can change that. But who we choose to be vulnerable with is much more selective.

I only want to trust people with my identity development who will improve me. Who is going to celebrate with me when I get a promotion? Who is going to slap sense into me when I'm being ridiculous? Who will bring me ice cream when I'm sad and push me to dream bigger while coasting aimlessly through life? I want people around me who actually pray for me when I ask them to and follow up with me to witness the miracles. I need people I can be honest with when I feel like venting or want validation.

Having good people like that in my close circle makes life incredible. A circle like that is a fortress. I am safe to feel, risk, and rest when I have good friends around me. Great relationships get sweeter with time. The more we learn about one another, the more we can encourage one another to our highest potential. Happy people view life as long and sweet. The people around us are what help us see life that way. They bring happiness by providing meaning and connection to every moment.

We can't know how many days we will be on this earth. Hopefully, we get a long time. But life can be sweet whether our bodies carry us one more day or another few decades. Surround yourself with people who make every day an adventure and every heartache worth it. Get honest with the people who make you want to be better. Love somebody who respects your values and treasures your personality. There's only one of you. You are so special. You should be with people who can see that about you; it's your choice. Be loving toward anyone, but be picky with who you let change you. You are a unicorn, and you need Ashlyns to remind you of the truth.

LESSON 11

One of my best friends, Tori, took me and a couple of others wedding dress shopping with her. Being the girly girl I am, I looked forward to spending the day surrounded by lace and satin. A rambunctious older Italian woman owned one of the bridal stores we had an appointment at. Her energy and complimentary champagne elevated the hype of the experience far beyond the previous store. She talked before, during, and after each dress, but I loved hearing her stories.

She told us how she dated exclusively tall blond men until she fell in love with her now short, Spanish husband. None of her friends understood what she could be attracted to after her dating record of model men. But she knew it was love. Decades later, she professed confidence in her decision and gratefulness for the generations of family they've raised together. One of my friends noted, "Perfect is relative."

Perfect is relative. I don't identify as a perfectionist, but I've been accused of being one more than once. I admit my standards are high, and my ambitions are idealistic. Perfection has never been the goal for me, though. I just want what is best. When I heard my friend remark on the relativity of it, it resonated in my soul.

My best friend is marrying her perfect man. They support each other, admire one another, respect each other, and complement one another. Her ideal man is not anything like my ideal man. I don't want her "perfect." I want what and who is perfect for me.

I could hear the Italian woman rambling in the background about how finding the perfect dress is like finding the perfect man. When you find one you love, you stop kissing other boys; when you find the one you love, you stop trying on different dresses.

I started to wonder. What would perfect look like for me right now? What's my perfect life, job, Sunday, community, relationship, and home? And is it enough for me to enjoy those things the way I want them, even if no one else thinks they're perfect? Can I still go after what I want, even if it's only perfect to me?

Expectations can be a heavy load, especially when expectations that don't resonate with you are placed on you. Some expectations are explicit, but many are more understood. When I worked in college ministry, I remember how many students struggled to integrate their parents' expectations with their emerging identities. It's a tall order. We've got to find out what to do with expectations placed on us that may not necessarily be the best for us.

I fell in love, in my heart of hearts, with one of the wedding dresses my friend tried on. If I had her body and it was my special day, I wouldn't try on another dress. And while she looked breathtaking, she looked like she was wearing a dress I would want to wear. Later that day, she glowed when she tried on the perfect dress for her. It didn't just fit her body. It fit her personality and her vision for her wedding, and we could see the light in her eyes.

If I pushed my expectations of the perfect dress on my friend, she might not have ended up with her perfect dress. Even if she did, she might have had doubts or fears of disappointment because of what I wanted. I would hate for my selfishness or preferences even slightly to dim the glow of this exciting experience. She knew who she was, what she wanted, and what felt best. When she knew, we all felt it, too. She was undeniably perfect, and I couldn't be happier for her.

The more we embrace ourselves, the more we learn our preferences. The more we know our preferences, the more we temper others' expectations. The more we temper others' expectations, the more choices we make that we want. The more choices we make, the more we embrace ourselves. This is how we build identity. We may try on many fabulous dresses before we find the one we want to take home. We might even be convinced we've found the right one until we find the "righter" one. But we've got to be true to the things that fit our personalities, our visions for our lives, and make us glow.

I could see my friend's face when she would walk out in a gorgeous dress that wasn't *the* dress. Little cues helped me discern if she thought the dress was great or not great and if she was trying to talk herself into something. When she tried on an extraordinary dress, she would dance around giddily. There was no hiding what she loved, and we all knew it.

Keep the people around who know what you're like when you're happy and content. Keep the people who will call your bluff when you're talking yourself into something that might be great but isn't you. Keep the people who know your style and vision for your future, who won't let you sell yourself short or go broke trying to achieve a particular look. Keep the people who will spend the day acting like it's their first glass of champagne and not the fourth, like it's the first dress you've tried on each time and not the twelfth, and like the big decisions are meaningful moments they wouldn't pass up for the world.

Tori's the friend who drives over to sit on the couch by me when I'm in the worst pain and can't be alone. She's one of the few I trust with the gritty details of the worst moments of my life. I know she'd go to hell and back for me.

Having talked me off metaphorical cliffs many times in the years of our friendship, Tori is protective. But even with this maternal quality, she isn't overbearing. Tori, gracious as Jesus, taught me a fundamental truth about loving people well. She told me that we like to have a grip on the people we care about. When someone we love has been hurt, we tend to hold them even tighter to keep them from getting hurt again. But this grasp squeezes the life out of people. Life isn't meant to be treated like that.

If we love someone, we have to hold them with open hands. We have to give them the agency and support to create the life they want, even if it risks hurt. Love is not control. Control is an empty substitute for love. Tori trusting me to make my own decisions for my life makes me think more about what I want. I realized the way I live my life is going to, directly and indirectly, affect the people who care about me. I don't want to live like I'm alone in a vacuum. I want to honor the people who love me by living well.

Have you ever wondered why people have expectations for you? Why does your mom ask when you'll have kids, and the elders at church ask when you get married? What if they aren't trying to nag? What if the root of their questions is an expression of care? In some way, the people who expect things from you expect it because they think you're capable of it and maybe even care for you.

Some people will have their expectations for you to live vicariously through you or simply because they have too many judgments in their hearts. That's on them. Others will have expectations for you, like a coach or mentor, that will push you toward your highest potential. Others will have expectations for you because they need you to come through for them.

Expectations aren't bad things, but they aren't the gods of your life. You might need to break free of some expectations. You might need to embrace some of them. Choose for yourself. Think for yourself. For all our best efforts to care for one another well, hold each other accountable to our potential, and communicate expectations, the most important conversation about how you live is between you and God.

I don't want to waste my life people-pleasing. No matter how hard I try to outgrow those tendencies, another layer follows. This isn't the time to give in. Day by day, I will lay down what other people think is perfect for me and follow the only One who is in every way perfect. He can give me what is perfect for me and make me perfect for whatever circumstance I find myself in. I don't want to waste my friendships trying to control. I want to trust God to be perfect for them as well. Once, Jesus commanded us to be perfect as our Father in heaven is perfect. All our best intentions and strongest friendships couldn't manufacture godlike perfection. Only One can, and that's Jesus. He's all we need to find our perfect.

LESSON 12

My maternal grandfather is a spectacular man. He was married to my grandmother for over half a century until she passed. He's a brilliant businessman and an exceptional family man. My earliest memories with him are coated in the eager anticipation for handspun milkshakes after dinner. My childhood is sprinkled with fall Saturdays screaming at the TV while the Georgia Bulldogs played their hearts out, then attempting an equally vicious game out in the yard. He'd put on the best Fourth of July parties with the most fantastic fireworks shows over the lake. Every greeting I can recall from him has been a hug and a kiss on the head. I'm so grateful to have men like him around me.

Besides all the fun he's brought into my life, he also has that quintessential grandfather wisdom. While I've been able to glean some nuggets of truth in some of our conversations, a lot I learn from him comes through conversations he has with my mom that I hear about down the line. One of the most recent ones is that problems don't get better with age.

I'm a wine girl. I'm not a huge wine girl, but I enjoy trying new kinds socially or drinking a glass while I cook a nice meal. The thing about wine is that the finest are aged; they get better with time.

I would love it if problems got better with time. Problems are not wine, though. Problems sour like dairy. I have a friend who experienced some intense trauma growing up and repressed it as a means of self-preservation. Given the resources and knowledge at that age, I would've done the same. Unfortunately, repression did not cause the trauma to resolve—neither did the distance from the people involved or time from the occurrence of pain. Symptoms like anxiety and ineffective coping mechanisms developed. Relationships strained under the weight of deeply tucked away pain. The more my friend desired to grow and heal, the more evidence of trauma appeared that needed to be addressed.

Great friendships, a great therapist, and a lot of prayer have gently uprooted lies in her belief system and helped integrate the trauma from where it was stored in the brain and body. That isn't a process that will unfold naturally. Trauma integration takes effort and a whole lot of grace for yourself. It also produces hope for the future and a sense of safety that we need to reach higher levels of self-actualization.

I like to think of problems in terms of their layers. The first layer of a problem that usually appears is the practical layer. Something dysfunctional has interrupted the flow of my life, so I can not move forward in practice healthily without addressing it. This could be a work problem, relationship problem, personal problem, purpose problem, cultural problem, etc. Let's say our practical layer is a lack of purpose. I wake up one day in a crisis. I don't know what I'm doing with my life or why I'm here. I am directionless and don't know what steps to take because no passion drives my momentum.

Now, I could pick a direction to take in life and run with it, but the purposelessness will likely continue. The next layer I want to acknowledge is the cognitive layer. In high school, a teacher taught me the difference between thinking and feeling. We often say "I feel like" or "I feel that," when we are talking about what we think. To articulate well (and to know ourselves well), we would do well to say more often what we think. "I feel like I should go back to school" or "I feel that this current situation doesn't make sense for me" are better represented as thoughts. Give your thoughts room to reason. "I think I should go back to school" opens the door for reasoning about the benefits and costs of that decision. Another great cognitive tool is a mind map. Start with a bubble in the center of a page and fill it with your practical problem. Draw a branch off of that bubble to a smaller bubble that is a smaller piece of the problem. Continue with branches and bubbles until you can see the problem in its entirety in front of you.

For example, the center bubble might say purposelessness. I would branch bubbles off of that like "going back to school," "asking for new responsibility at work," or "taking up a new hobby." My "going back to school" bubble might branch off into "tuition," "night vs day classes," "online vs in person." My "asking for new responsibility at work" bubble might branch into "gifts/strengths/skills I have to offer" and "needs in the office/community I'd like to meet." My "taking up a new hobby" bubble might branch off into "alone/group hobbies," "budget for a hobby," and "passion projects." You may be surprised how many opportunities present themselves when you allow your mind to be creative. Seeing options may also relieve any feelings of being stuck in your problem. This leads us to the next layer.

Following our thought layer is the emotional layer. I dwell a lot on this emotional layer. We pick up more baggage to carry forward when we push through problems without addressing our emotions. That's not necessary. This is the layer where we can use "I feel," only this time, we follow those words with a feeling. Developing language for your feelings is one of the greatest gifts you can give yourself. Most people dealing with a problem that I talk to communicate one (or more) of three feelings: sadness, anger, and fear. If you've ever seen a Feelings Wheel, you know we experience significantly more depth and detail in our emotions than just those three.

Caring for our emotions is like caring for a child. We have to figure out what's wrong and what we need. We have to tend to the body and the mind. Our emotions are neural firings. They are a brain-based process that everyone has. However, our emotional responses are typically in the brain's more "animalistic" part than the cognitive responses which are found in the more "reasonable" part. Emotions aren't only in our brains, though. If you think about the experience of intense emotions, we experience them in our whole bodies: weak knees, upset stomach, flushed skin, racing heartbeat, shaky hands, sweat, dry mouth, tears, choked-up sensation, etc. So, as we care for our emotions, we cannot separate the heart from the body. Diet, sleep, and exercise are the big three of physical health related to emotional health. Being too strict or lax in these categories can exacerbate our emotional state.

Many children grow up with a comfort item that aids in learning to self-soothe. Blankies, nightlights, and stuffed animals dominate this market. As adults, carrying our baby blankets would be off-putting, but that doesn't mean we do away with coping mechanisms entirely. Usually, people who aren't intentional to develop effective coping mechanisms end up using ineffective or even harmful ones. I have spent years learning my needs and finding effective sources of soothing. Some of mine include venting to close friends, asking for prayer, walking, crying, taking a hot shower, getting a massage, journaling, playing piano, etc. Generally, I can express strong emotions without repression or explosion because I know I am taken care of.

For purposelessness, I may start with my most overarching feeling. Am I sad, mad, or scared? If I'm scared, I explore what I'm scared of. *I am scared my life will be full of regrets. I am scared my partner won't be proud of me. I am scared I have nothing to offer the world.* That may lead to feelings of sadness, anger, or something entirely different to continue exploring. Once I've been honest about my feelings, usually in prayer or conversation with someone I trust, I tend to my body. Is my heart rate up? Is my jaw tense? Is my appetite gone? How can I nurture what my body needs to return to a calm and secure homeostasis?

Emotions aren't chronological or linear. We often have them in response to a stimulus, but they can reappear in what might seem like an illogical moment. Emotions aren't logical–don't force them to be. Show yourself patience and love. The more security you develop to experience and tend to your emotions, the better your relationship with your emotions will be.

The last layer of our problem that I'll talk about here is spiritual. There is a growing body of research on how impactful spirituality is to our well-being. We need to attend to the spiritual layer when we work toward solutions. Scripture shows evidence of the spiritual realm around us and that it interferes with our life experience. Paul the Apostle emphasizes the spiritual conflict we face over the natural conflict we see. Our spiritual layer is best cared for by the Spirit of God, whom Jesus sent to us as a Helper, Teacher, and Advocate. Prayer (or conversation with God) is vital to our problem-solving. Whether by miraculous intervention, supernatural peace, or inspired strategy, God can lead our spirits through any problems. Intentional surrender to His lordship and leadership through faith and trust will strengthen even the weariest parts of our spirits.

Problems are going to come and keep coming. As we grow in our capacity to address each layer of our problems, we will become more confident in problem-solving. Our problems may become more complex, but we can adapt. I would hate for someone to visit the metaphorical house of my life and be overwhelmed by the stench of soured problems. I don't even want to live in a house like that.

Relationships are like fine wine. When I get discouraged by my problems, I like to pour a metaphorical glass of wine and whine it out. My relationships with God, my pastor, my therapist, my parents, and my closest friends take the edge off the work it takes to tackle my problems. I can't depend on them to do all the work for me. Throwing myself into social activity or others' drama won't make mine go away. But having trusted relationships in my life is something to enjoy, no matter the circumstances. I want to work on the problems that come, knowing they'll go sooner or later. But I want to invest in the great things in life—the long-lasting love, the deep-meaning friendships, and the loving-kindness of God. Those will bring joy and memorable moments to my life as I carry on.

LESSON 13

I met with one of the leaders of a ministry in our church for a rudimentary check-in. We started talking about ministry but were quickly sidetracked talking about Margaret Kirkland. She told me Margaret Kirkland changed her life.

Margaret Kirkland changed my life, too. Not so much all at once but the gradual change from being seen and loved. I knew of Margaret through her son and daughter-in-law; I worked for them in my first years of ministry. When I started working as a pastor, I set up meetings with anyone in the church who might know anything about our church history and aspirations for community transformation. Margaret was one of those. Our conversation over lunch confirmed all the things I had heard about her. She is a wise, kind, gentle mother figure devoted to God, family, and the Church.

I'd prayed for months that God would bring a mentor into my life. I felt the inclination in my spirit that Margaret could be that for me. So, I asked her on the way back from the church if she would consider mentoring me. She asked if she could pray about it and that I would, too. We decided not long after to meet for coffee. Every few weeks, Margaret and I meet for coffee or tea somewhere in town. She asks about my life and tells me bits about hers. She encourages me, advises me, and prays for me. Margaret brought me one of my first meals when I moved into my new apartment. She continually lifts my spirit when I'm disappointed or anxious. She treats me with homemade birthday cakes and thoughtful Christmas gifts. Anytime I'm feeling off, Margaret's encouragement and powerful prayer are one text away.

Love like that shapes us. I'm grateful to Margaret for her generosity of heart and mind. My ministry leader is thankful to her, too. Margaret brought her into a more fantastic experience of the church family, Sunday after Sunday, showing her the love of Christ. As this leader shared her testimony of Margaret and other stories from her ministry, I felt amazed by the Church. People like that, welcoming those who need to be loved, are the ones who bring the Kingdom of Heaven to earth. They are vessels filled with the glory of God that instill hope into those of us who sometimes forget.

We are the Church, whether we are attending our community of faith on a Sunday morning or bringing a fresh meal to a young adult who is getting her footing in a new city. We forfeit the power of encouragement when we get wrapped up in life's busyness and everyday conversations' mundanity. Our words and actions can destroy, maintain, or create strength.

As the leader left my office, I told her how much I appreciated her. Something about our shared love for Margaret filled me with gratitude that I needed to express. It's like we had bonded over the shared treasure, Margaret Kirkland. Letting moments pass when we could say something kind is too easy. I don't want to be a person who flatters flippantly, but I especially don't want to be a person who lets moments pass when simple, kind words have a profound impact.

One of those moments happened to me a few years ago. I had always been big on writing people encouragement. One day, a buddy of mine came to my work table and sat beside me. I don't recall what he said, but I remember how his words made me feel. His gift of consideration, intentionality, and boldness affected me. I realized how impactful sitting across from someone to say good things about them can be. Our words don't have to be deep, meaningful, or elaborate to be healing and strengthening. Simple ones are enough.

Our pastor, Tom, reminds us frequently that anxiety and thanksgiving don't coexist in our brains. Thankfulness shifts the way we see the world. The effects of a grateful mindset can change our world, too. Imagine how different your sphere of influence would be if you thanked the people around you for the good impact they have. Acknowledgment gives people the strength to keep going. Growing weary of doing good is far too familiar, but encouraging people by expressing your thankfulness can be the boost they need. When we choose an attitude of appreciation and express our gratitude, we generate morale and deter anxiety from our environments. Being thankful benefits everyone.

Whenever a staff member resigns, we have a meal and share why we are thankful for them. This lightens the heaviness of their departures every time. And sometimes, we need to lighten up. I get bogged down with garbage throughout the day, and accepting that as part of life is easy. It is part of life. If we live a good life, we'll get other people's mess on us and probably make a few messes ourselves. Laughter is the perfect medicine for that. Every once in a while, I like to thank God for the mess. It's okay to sit back with God and chuckle at the glass onion of humanity.

People who can't take themselves lightly bring weight wherever they go. We aren't those people. We get to be the ones in the world but not of the world, part of the system but not controlled by the system, in the mess but not defined by the mess. Thankfulness lightens our spirits. We remember the gifts God has given us in relationships, virtues, and materials. If you go to impoverished countries, you can witness the power of gratitude firsthand. Someone with so little may invite you into their home with a beaming smile and all they have to offer laid out on the table for you. They'll tell you how grateful they are you came by. If you're like me, moments like that keep you from going home the same person you were when you came. True gratitude is humbling and perspective-shifting; it's world-changing.

God's will for us is constant thanksgiving because of the work of Christ. In all things, we can choose thankfulness and mean it. Jesus' death and resurrection claimed peace in our hearts. No matter what we face, we have access to inner stability and rest because of Him. The instruction in Scripture to give thanks is repetitive. From the looks of it, our gratitude is not dependent on our circumstances or feelings toward them. Gratitude is a constant in response to the generosity and love of God.

I don't know about you, but that challenges me. I don't always feel grateful. How can I reconcile the command to be thankful at all times with transparency before God about my true feelings? The power of the Gospel and the gift of grace are the answer. The reality of eternal life in Christ and the merciful nearness of God to us now builds my hope.

I'm not saying look away from what's in front of you. I'm asking you to broaden your perspective to the complete picture of what's happening in your life. God is not going to abandon you. He won't leave you hopeless. Thankfulness is difficult when our feelings distort the truth that He is with us. He is for you. He is writing and perfecting your story. That's real. That's true. It's not the nature of humanity to thank God when times are tough. But it's the nature of our spirits to praise Him when standing on the truth of our redemption.

A glaringly apparent difference between me and Paul the Apostle is that I am not thankful in all circumstances. My hope in Christ is that I could be. We didn't see Jesus model thanksgiving when He was in the Garden of Gethsemane or on the way to the Cross. We didn't see it when He was on the Cross. He's overwhelmed with sorrow and speaks very little. Then Paul comes along as an apostle of Christ and reiterates the importance of thanksgiving in all circumstances. Seems a little fishy to me. I don't think the example of Jesus and the instruction of Paul contradict. Paul was acquainted with suffering, so it's not as if he's ignorant. Jesus was God in the flesh, so it's not as if He was missing the mark.

Jesus modeled suffering, sorrow, and pain as God who passionately desires connection with us. Paul testifies of that extravagant love and clarifies the appropriate response. We don't have to dance on graves to be obedient Christians. We can cry at the tombs of our own Lazarus' but still rejoice in the gift of Life and the power of the Spirit like Christ did. Those have a direct impact on our circumstances. The duality of temporary tragedy with eternal life allows for overwhelming sorrow and constant gratitude. Our souls are stretched and shaped into the likeness of Christ. You can have both. I may even dare to say your portion is both, at least for now. We have trouble in this world, but we also have peace. Please give yourself grace as you learn to live like Jesus with all the instructions of Scripture. I'm convinced the gift of gratitude makes all that is complicated a little simpler.

LESSON 14

Perseverance permeates Scripture. Moses contended for Israel's freedom, Jesus asked the disciples to pray all night in the Garden of Gethsemane, and Paul and James reiterated its importance. Numerous passages encourage us not to give up. Some days, this is easier said than done.

A fundamental aspect of perseverance is faithfulness. I am fueled to persevere when I consider what lengths God has gone for me. He has never given up on me. His faithfulness to me is the measure I can extend back to Him and out to others. I have seen pure faithfulness from Him firsthand and know the One who sustains faithfulness personally. If I want to know how to do the same, I simply have to ask. I can love this way because He loved me first. He is the source of my love, faithfulness, and perseverance.

Over and over, Jesus invites us to go with Him and minister to people. We need dedication for this. We can choose to follow Him or follow something else. The religion that Jesus wants us to ascribe to is caring for those struggling and hurt. As followers of Christ, we are obligated to those suffering. Obligation tends to carry a pressured or shameful connotation in our culture. For now, let's pretend it isn't a bad thing.

Imagine you're in a crowded mall. You hear the chatter of numerous conversations all at once. If you don't watch where you're going, you might bump into a stranger. You're on your way into a store when you witness an older woman's purse being stolen. The woman screams for her belongings as the thief runs off. The room is still for a moment. The woman starts to look around the room, and one by one, each person turns to avoid eye contact with her. She meets your gaze for a brief second. Do you look away? Keep walking? Ask her how she's doing? Stay with her? For how long?

The Bystander Effect is a social phenomenon in which all witnesses avoid the responsibility of what they've witnessed, committed to the belief that another witness will step up to help. It's easy to assume someone else will always do the right thing, but this selfishness and apathy isolate people in need.

In our relationship with God, we can repress the obligations arising in us by convincing ourselves that someone else will intervene. We tell people we will be praying for them instead of taking a moment to minister to them. We keep our windows rolled up at the intersections where impoverished individuals beg for money. We ignore the staff member in the building who is used to being overlooked. We assume others will advocate for societal changes that are needed. We stay quiet in group settings where a little honesty could have a significant impact for the better.

Meeting the needs of every person around us could become incredibly exhausting. There's just not enough time in the day to solve all the world's problems, even the ones directly in front of us. The healing and help our world desires require strategy, longevity, and intentionality; they require faithfulness. So, do we quit our day jobs to become humanitarians? Do we repress pity and guilt when we pass by someone who is hurting?

What if we exchange the belief that someone else will intervene with the belief that we are equipped and possibly called to intervene? We interact with the world from a position of power, resources, wisdom, and favor. Because we are of the Spirit of God and created in the image of God, we all have access to His justice and His compassion in us. Numbing the desire to influence the world with the love of God numbs our connection with God. Our influence is a part of Himself that He has given us. Through Christ, we carry authority everywhere we go. We have to decide what to do with that authority.

Maslow's Hierarchy of Needs is a social theory proposing five innate needs: physiological, safety, love and belonging, esteem, and self-actualization. The first need includes food, water, air, shelter, sleep, clothing, and reproduction. The second covers resources, health, property, employment, and personal security. The third addresses intimacy, friendship, family, and the sense of connection. The fourth encompasses respect, self-esteem, strength, status, freedom, and recognition. The fifth entails the desire to become the best one can be. When I learned about this theory, a whole treasure chest of ways to use my God-given inheritance opened up.

As I read the Word, I see how intentionally God desires to meet every one of our needs. He is a good Father. Throughout Scripture, we can understand God as a Provider and Protector. Knowing His Word is wonderful because it reveals His heart. Creation's food, clothing, and shelter come from God. He gives us rest and sweet sleep. He made healing available to us through the Cross. He orchestrates paths and destinies. God brought us into His family. Jesus claims us as His friends. He constantly extends His connection to us. He redefined us as conquerors and co-heirs, made entirely free by grace. Through hope, mercy, and renewing our minds, He creates pathways for us to become perfect like He is. He knows what we need.

Before Maslow ever suggested how we experience lack, God provided for our needs and sustained our existence. This is a testimony of His faithfulness to be active in our lives. He created an environment for us to thrive in the security of His promises. We don't have to worry or envy because He's our caretaker.

I understand there are times when these promises seem distant. I've been through periods of life where I felt like I didn't have enough; I felt like I was lacking. In those uncertain times, I want to align my beliefs with the reality of His care for me over the circumstances of my discomfort. This kind of faith is possible because He is faithful. He always has been and He always will be. His faithfulness to me includes the times He led me out of tight spots and provided for my needs but ultimately rests on what Jesus did through His death and resurrection.

The Cross is the final word. I used to think that meant that I needed to shut up about my ifs, whens, and buts. But the final word of the Cross silenced the enemy and made a way for me to come before Him in confidence. The Cross isn't God's way of shutting us down when we can't see His faithfulness. It's a pillar of the heights and depths of His love for us. It's a sign that He holds the victory. It's a promise that we will be made whole. It's an assurance that no angel, demon, future, power, spirit, life, or death could separate us from His love.

The Good News is that He made this confidence and assurance available to everyone. My testimony of His faithfulness and acceptance of His generosity allows me to bring others into His security. I don't have to give from my lack or need. I don't need to exhaust myself from caring for people from my strength. He gave everything; I freely received everything. Then, I freely give everything. This truth makes cheerful giving easy. When the Spirit persuades us to sacrifice what we have for someone else, we can feel joy because we are saving someone without really missing out on anything significant ourselves. Jesus is it, He's everything, He's all. We've got Him. We are covered.

The instruction to love our neighbor as yourself is well-known. Generally, we can look around to see who is running themselves into the ground loving others more than themselves versus who is running others into the ground loving themselves more. The balance is tricky if you're trying to share God's love apart from knowing God's love. I think that's why God said He turns away evildoers who do the same actions He loves for us to do. They do it apart from Him. We're hurting ourselves and others when we try to love out of only the love we generate. Our love doesn't cut it. Manufactured just can't measure up to the real thing. Loving God with all parts of our being infuses each part of us with His love for us. Our relationship with Him is vital for meeting the needs in the world that people are desperate to meet.

As we grow in love for God and, ultimately, His love for us, we begin a natural flow of releasing the resources of heaven to a needy world. It's funny how things fall into place when we put God first. Regular ministry is no longer a task or taxing but a consistent expression of our relationship with Him. Faithfulness is the fruit of the Spirit, the byproduct of abiding in Him.

Praying through Maslow's hierarchy of needs is a great start for practically aligning your beliefs with the reality of God's faithfulness. Assess with God where you're at and what you still need. Ask God to show you He cares for you in your most insecure areas. Meditate on verses affirming He will give you precisely what you need. Then, follow the Spirit into opportunities He provides for you to receive what He has for you.

One of the first lies fed to humanity was that God withholds from us. You cannot eat the fruit from that tree; it's off-limits. Thoughts and beliefs that God withholds from you should frustrate you; they should not sit well in your spirit because they are twisted truths. God says yes sometimes and no other times. I won't pretend like I understand why. But He will always be faithful to you. You can leave mistrust in God at the door and fully embrace, in a leap of faith, that He will eternally be your good Father; you're going to be okay. This faith isn't a name-it and claim-it manifesting type of faith. This faith is available to us because of God's grace. His favor, His covenant with us, allows us to believe that He is going to be faithful to us like He said He would be.

When you talk about what you still need with God, glance at what you have and what you have in excess. What can you begin to give away freely? If you've got extra food in your house, pack some meals to give out as you drive to work. If you have a lot on your plate at work and the freedom to delegate, empower someone to work with you. If you are a chatty person, connect with someone with social anxiety. If you're super confident, teach people how to feel good in their skin. Pull others up with you on whatever ladder of success matters to you.

We can be creative in how we minister God's love to people. The important thing is that we love with what God has given us to do it. The faithful love necessary to change the world is a gift God releases in and through you. All you have to do is ask. He's that good.

LESSON 15

The beauty of perseverance is that it matures us; it helps us become complete. The parts of you and me that are raw, missing, or unformed come together over time. We can dig up pieces of ourselves in new environments and uncover strengths within us that may only come into the light through challenges.

Some people believe personalities are fixed, but I see us as ever-evolving. A fundamental part of our biology is that we adapt to our environments. We undergo thousands of adaptations between social, emotional, physical, and spiritual environments in which we oscillate and move across our whole lives. Our commitment to resilience determines the quality of our changes in each setting.

We change in places we stay still, like trees in the forest and rocks by the seashore. Trees become more of what they already are. They get taller, stronger, and broader. They provide shade, oxygen, and sustenance for wildlife. They reproduce. In the same way, we develop into more of ourselves when we stay in an environment, and we can influence others in our unique ways.

Rocks weather in water over time. Their minerals are slowly chipped away by the elements and carried into new places. They dissolve and evaporate, becoming rain somewhere the rock would never see. Similarly, we are nicked and eroded by our environments. They take pieces of us through pain and loss, carrying the essence of our beliefs and values to places beyond our reach. Hints of what we live to show the world trickle down from the sky in far-off places combined with countless others' values. We never need to underestimate the impact we have around us. Your presence changes how things would have happened had you not been there.

We also change in new places. I'm sure we've all reconnected with friends we haven't seen in years. Though they're familiar, some things will inevitably be different. Their new friends, new schedule, and maybe even new diet can cause subtle changes that amount to something over time. We spend time overseas and come back with new worldviews that change how we interact or make decisions. We gain new skills and interests that shift our personalities a degree or two at a time.

We change in terrible environments. Sad or bad events occur, and we can overcome them or be overtaken by them. I never want to be overtaken entirely. I have an inherent value worth preserving; so do you. Giving up is more often rooted in the hopelessness of our perceptions than the impossibility of a resolution. Terrible environments test our character and refine us. We grow and protect hope as we persevere in the environments that scare us the most. Granted, sometimes we can and need to leave dangerous environments. But there are some unavoidable, uncomfortable places we will find ourselves in throughout life that we may just have to endure.

One of the first big things that changed me was how often I moved. New environments unlocked new parts of me I didn't expect. I'm in my late twenties, moving into my seventeenth home. Moving so much convinced me I had a fear of commitment. I thought that about myself for a long time. Maybe I couldn't stay in one place for over a year or two. I got great at making new friendships. I developed a deep wound from saying so many goodbyes. I had a hard time relating to people who were upset that their parents were selling their childhood homes; I had no basis to grasp that kind of loss. I had no desire to settle down in the future or buy a home. It seemed odd to spend hundreds of thousands or get trapped in a mortgage when the next ten years are so unpredictable.

I like to imagine who I might have been if I didn't move so much. Maybe I would have childhood friends who are still my closest circle. I'd be more cautious in new situations and less adventurous in my travels. Goodbyes would hurt differently, and I would have probably compiled a lot more junk in my house over the years. But because I moved a lot, I love meeting new people and visiting new places. I know what I like in a city and a home. I'm more secure in my faith than in my environment because environments change, but God stays constant. I'm way more relaxed than I was ten years ago because of my friendships and the people who have invested in me from all over. I love who I am and what I do. I couldn't have made it here without the people I met in different places I called home. Many of the moves I lived through I wouldn't have chosen. But they got me here, and I'm thankful for that.

Another significant change was my parents' divorce. It happened well over a decade ago. I still feel ripple effects far removed from the event itself. Outside of the deaths of relatives, my parents' divorce was the biggest tragedy I experienced firsthand. Divorces can be, maybe all are, terrible environments socially. Relationships are tense, awkward, aggravated, and desperate for security and belonging. I was twelve when it happened. I needed to learn to navigate having two homes, two churches, two friend groups, and two very different parents as primary caregivers depending on which house I was at that day, without dividing myself into two separate people. I had to start dating after watching my most significant romantic relationship to model dissolve. I still have to figure out how to divide my vacation days between holidays with mom, holidays with dad, holidays with friends, and time to do what I want.

Imagining who I would be without the divorce feels more of a mystery than if I hadn't moved so often. The divorce broke me into pieces that God, friends, and family filled with love. Now I have a higher capacity to withstand pain, more trust in my support system, more compassion for people who suffer, more understanding for other people's decisions that impact my life, more natural ability to invite people into family-like relationships, and more conviction that God can redeem our worst moments. I'd love to see what my family could have become if we stayed a unit and made it through the challenging parts. But I'm also content and grateful for my family now. I love the redemptive story God orchestrated through our mistakes. I want to keep living in this one because He has made it beautiful.

I lived in Athens, Georgia, for five years. I was so proud to have stayed in one place for that long. I did have four different homes throughout those five years, but leases and roommates changed a lot in college towns. My five years in Athens caused a significant transformation in my life. It was like an incubator for my development. I transferred to the University of Georgia, so I already had a good grip on living away from home, paying bills, and creating the kind of life I wanted to live in a new city. I chose my major, Human Development and Family Sciences, in Athens. I loved what I studied. I got certificates in Emotional Intelligence,

Family Life Education, and Arch Ready Professionalism. I spent three years on staff at a campus ministry. In those three years, I took a long, hard look at my identity and influence, and learned how to implement those into life wherever I go. I had a couple of significant relationships and went on many dates to discover what I liked and didn't like in romantic relationships. I met some of my best friends there. I mentored some college students who inspired me to write my first book, which I published right before moving to Atlanta.

I would be entirely different if I hadn't stayed in Athens. I would still be questioning myself and second-guessing my decisions. I'd be insecure in social settings and most likely working in a field I didn't enjoy as much. I might have even stayed in one of my earlier relationships, which would make me a very different woman than I am now. I wouldn't be as confident in my leadership or probably love how God made me as much. I'd be in bad shape without the strong women in my close circle now and the incredible men who have supported me throughout the years since I met them in Athens.

I chose to plant myself in Athens when I moved there. Looking back, I'm so proud of myself and all I accomplished. I'm thankful for who I've become. I'm amazed at all God did in and through me. Now, it's a goal of mine to let my roots go as deep as they can as fast as they can for however long I am in one place because the fruit of what God produces in me is so sweet and sustaining for me and the people around me.

I've seen a lot of change in the short time I've been alive. In hindsight, I can see the abundance of God's mercy toward me. Through every event, He has sustained, protected, grown, provided, and refined me. He has brought redemption to parts of my story I didn't expect ever to love. Trusting Him throughout the different circumstances strengthened my character and fortified my hope. Even when things seem hopeless, I can't silence the hope He has carved into my nature through my experiences. In light of this, letting the world determine who I am or become would be unnatural. I've seen what He and I can do when we partner together.

Seeing how good He's been to me is something I crave and am filled with over and over. Time is on my side when it comes to fulfilling His promises to me. I'm not going to run out of time before I see Him come through for me. I want to surrender the control of outcomes, the preferences for my environment, and the development of my identity to Him because He can make all things beautiful in time. I can't without Him.

As I trust Him, I gain a greater perspective on life through every change. I attain more understanding that His loving-kindness toward me is relentless. The knowledge of God, more than anything else, changes me. It changes my mind to hold onto hope, lean into perseverance, embrace change, and become better than I dreamed I could be.

LESSON 16

A group of people from multiple churches gathered to discuss worship as a touchpoint with each other between their regular worship gatherings. Some friends of mine had been a part of the group since the beginning and invited me. Over the years, their worship nights have collected people with a passion for worship and given them community. They have witnessed countless testimonies of people encountering God personally and spent countless hours blessing the Lord with praise.

As one of the newest in the group, I did not know what to expect. I have been a part of worship teams and gatherings most of my life in many different contexts. Sometimes, the only similarity is that we worship the same God. The music, dancing, and art style reflect the culture of the unique individuals who make it up. For this meeting, a leader split us into groups and assigned us passages of Scripture.

Each Scripture had to do with worship in some way or another. We had five minutes to read the verses, discussing their meaning and how they applied to us. When our time concluded, we went around the room sharing what we learned. One group shared about when King David dancing naked in the streets. This stuck out to me. Our worship leader sang about the same passage of Scripture earlier that day in worship at my church service. Then, a question resonated within me. *When was the last time you did something foolish?*

My core is a wide-eyed and open-hearted child. But the older I get, the more pressure I feel to avoid looking childish. I have learned to rationalize, weigh costs and benefits, and anticipate the consequences of my actions. While these have helped me become a more responsible adult and efficient employee, they confined the wild love and faith in me.

When I was younger, I used to generously give my money to needs I came across. Most of my money was given to me around birthdays, holidays, or the bit I made working at a pizza shop. This generosity habit continued through college and a few years after. I never had a bill go unpaid and freely gave when I felt the Holy Spirit prompt me. A couple of years ago, fear crept into my heart and made a home there. I budgeted my giving allowance and rarely gave a penny more. Blessing others became less fun and more of a financial burden. Being a cheerful giver is hard when you're stressed about giving. What started as stewarding my finances well became a dependency on my budget rather than my Provider. I am trying to be a little more generous with my money because it's not mine. It is what God has given me to use how He wants me to. Whether giving it to my apartment complex to honor my agreement with them, to a missionary who needs it to live out their calling, or to bless a friend, I am channeling resources freely to the world around me.

When I was younger, I used to dance. I am a terrible dancer. Watching me dance is like watching a baby deer try to stand for the first time. But I used to love the movement and the feel of music flowing through my body. The older I got, the more self-aware and subsequently insecure I became. For a while I rarely danced, even to be goofy in the privacy of my own home. Life is more fun when you dance. It's an exercise in letting go and letting loose. I want to be more relaxed and fun. Taking myself too seriously is a waste of life and bad for my overall well-being. A lousy dancer is often just as fun to watch, anyway.

Some people are old souls. The cores of their beings are comfort and quiet where I have cravings for adventure and wonder. One is not better than the other. A lot of my friends balance me out with that old-soul approach to life. My caution for all of us is this: don't let your preferences limit you. Just because you prefer to be observant or reserved doesn't mean you can't join in on the fun. If you want to, you can be goofy and silly. If you want to, you can be loud and wild. If you want to, you can be spontaneous and fun.

But if you don't want to, don't. Sometimes we let our personalities define our actions.

For me, it's the opposite. I like to be having fun loudly and running around to see the world. I used to think I couldn't enjoy quiet alone time at home because it's not my personality. I'd anxiously fill minute by minute of my day so I could make the most out of each one. Then when I absolutely had to be home, I'd rest up as quickly as I could to get moving again. I loved this pace of life. Unfortunately, it's not too sustainable. Everybody needs time in stillness and silence.

I challenged myself one evening. Why couldn't I try out being quiet and alone for one evening? Just because I've been one way doesn't mean I can't be another. Since that evening, I've learned that I love quiet time alone. I don't love it in large doses, but I look forward to the bits of it carved into my days now. I'm getting to evolve, reaping all the benefits introverts have treasured for ages before I came along.

The thing that drew me to love quiet alone time? It wasn't stretching my personality or a dare to be different. It wasn't force or pressure. It was love. The two things I love most are God and relationships. (My dog is in the "relationships" category for better or for worse. I probably talk to him more than anyone else.) While I love enjoying time with God and people together, I started wanting time alone with God. Something in me needed to sneak away and be with Him.

Love is the strongest motivator I know. Love leads us to do things that we wouldn't normally do, say things we wouldn't normally say, and find ourselves in places where we wouldn't normally go. Love will have us surprising ourselves. Loving someone or something good will lead us to greater things than we ever dreamed for ourselves.

One of my favorite hymns is *Come Thou Fount*. In the final stanza, the lyrics are "bind my wandering heart to Thee." I pray this over myself all the time. I want my heart to be bound to God's always. When I think about how small and simple humanity is in the grand scheme of the cosmos, I wonder what could possibly be strong enough to bind our wandering spirits to the Divine. Only love.

Self-effort could never accomplish what love naturally produces in us. I'm not likely to dance in public. But if a song I love comes on, I just might. And if someone I love asks me to dance with them there, I wouldn't think twice. I'm not likely to give money to random people I pass during my day. But if I see a need, I just might. And if someone I love needs help, I wouldn't think twice.

We can try to change ourselves and our relationships until we run ourselves into the ground. We may see progress for a while, but we are guaranteed to burn out without love. Love is the mystical, powerful string that ties me to Divinity in this life. I am grounded, expanded, and fulfilled by it.

Loving God, life, and others isn't all moonlight and roses. Realistically, great love sees more days of quiet faithfulness than romantic whirlwinds. But the whirlwinds come. When they do, embrace them. When the joy of your salvation is as bright as the dawn, celebrate. When the colors of your life are brighter, enjoy. When the people around you fill your heart with gladness, take comfort. These are the blessings from the Fountain of Heaven.

Free yourself from the confines of mundanity when your heart is aching for something new. Let love flow in and through you. Let it motivate you and connect you to the beauty that God has made. I promise you'll be able to look back over the years at these heights of love and be filled with gratitude. Then, hope will fill the present moment, and perseverance will be about more than surviving. It will be a confident pursuit of the best part of life: being in love.

LESSON 17

Ecclesiastes 3 is one of my favorite passages in Scripture: everything made beautiful in its time, eternity written on our hearts, a time for this and a time for that. We talk about "seasons" in the church world a lot—maybe too much. The term has bugged me because we have four seasons in the physical realm, and they alternate with predetermined certainty. Apart from the occasional false early springs and winters in Georgia weather, I know summer will follow spring, fall-summer, winter-fall, and spring-winter. Our "seasons of the soul" are not as predictable and, perhaps, not the best descriptors. Ecclesiastes lends beautiful language for the same experiences. "A time for" suits well. With no predetermined start or end, you just know when you're in it.

For the longest time, I discerned a time of silence. I hadn't had many opportunities for large platforms, and the ones presented to me felt off-limits in my spirit. I'd speak here and there at little events where I felt permission to share, but none of the teachings felt remarkable. Even in conversations with friends, churchgoers, and strangers, I'd feel an internal hesitation to share everything I thought.

This hasn't always been the case for me. In my last "season," I embraced assertiveness with boldness. I felt the opportunity and permission to be forthright and "in the spotlight." Public speaking brought me joy and excitement. I aspired to grow in my speaking abilities and reach more people. I can't pinpoint the moment that changed, but looking back, I can see how different I was.

One of the sweetest changes since silence came is having secrets with God. I don't feel obligated to give everything away immediately like I used to. If I learn something with God as I read the Bible or feel Him impress something on my spirit for someone, I don't feel the pressure to tell them. A couple of years ago, I would have thought I was selfish for withholding. I thought I had an obligation to share what I thought was godly insight. But these secrets with God increased my dependence on Him. I learned to trust He will work in and through me and lead me to share when I need to. Silence expands my capacity for faith and hope. I hold onto the whispers of God in quiet expectation until I see Him fulfill what He has spoken (or correct my misunderstanding).

Have you ever had a friend self-sabotage, and know there's nothing you can say to stop them? You can see every step of the way how they are about to shoot themselves in the foot, they're shooting themselves in the foot, they're complaining that their foot hurts. I wish I could say I turned my concern into intercession. Unfortunately, my conversations with God about those times are more judgmental and frustrated on my end than compassionate. With far more grace than I had shown, God convicted me that I'm not quite the praying woman I think of myself as. I love to talk to God throughout my day and make time to listen, but I rarely intercede for others. I replaced opportunities to connect with God and cover the people I love by taking God's place of authority so I could judge how I wanted. What a bummer. In all my self-righteousness, I built up grievances that desperately needed a place to go. I decided to lay those down, along with my judgments and frustrations.

My frustrated prayers softened into heavy-hearted petitions. Slowly, they progressed into compassionate intercession and hopeful expectation. The closer I came to the heart of the Father for my friends, the more I could see the self-righteousness I had been caught in. I am eager to be pure but stubborn in acknowledging my faults. God's gentle hand removed me from the gunk I stood in and pulled me closer to Him. I received more of His loving-kindness for my friends and, in doing so, for me. I realized how lost I had been before.

A word at the wrong time can hurt the person we intend to help. Cycles of codependency occur insidiously when we get in the habit of "rescuing." Sometimes I need to be silent so I'm not upstaging God as the story's Hero. I need to trust that He saves, and others need to see it, too. Sure, He may use me to help at times. But God gets to make the call on how involved I get to be.

Jesus lived with unparalleled dependence on the Father (a perk of being God in the flesh). He seemed comfortable and confident doing all and only what the Father wanted Him to do. He healed, taught, ate, and napped in the peace of knowing the will of God for His life. No wonder He taught us to pray with reverence for the Father and His will. The more I grow in faith, the more I hope to live utterly and defenselessly dependent on God. I'd love not to be afraid of what people think or feel the need to explain myself. I dream of trusting the Spirit so confidently that I don't second-guess myself or wait to understand before I obey.

Silence shut off the sound of my voice so I could hear the voice of God. One of the simple relationship-savers many are familiar with now is active listening. Counselors teach us to listen and respond rather than monologue and react. I realize the same advice can save my ministry and strengthen my relationship with God. I want every conversation I'm a part of to include God, and I want to defer to His will over my agenda. Honestly, it's hard to admit I have an agenda. I see how arrogant I've been to assume I don't. The more I sit quietly with God, the more I see how different His voice is from mine. He is much more patient and slow to anger. His truth is more prosperous and received with joy or awe. I'm all about intervention to stop harmful behavior, but His intervention restores to a whole that is better than before.

With the awareness that I was generally in a time of silence, I learned to wait on God for times to speak. One of my friends calls this the "Spirit's nudging." The Spirit's nudging starts with the belief that God speaks to us. As we grow in the knowledge of His character and understanding of His Word, we grow in the awareness of His will for us. The Old and New Testaments help us know who God is and what He asks of us. We can determine what's right and wrong by studying the Bible. His Spirit in us helps us know who He is to us and what He is asking of us, specifically in a given moment. The Bible didn't tell me to go to graduate school or not, move into the apartments I've lived in, or date the guys I've dated. Neither did a voice in the sky. I had to trust the Spirit, nudging my spirit into making those choices and continuing to trust Him daily. Over time, discernment has grown in me through the Spirit.

After a long time of silence, I began to feel nudged to speak. I spoke at an event and felt more nudges to speak up in conversations. Even the renewed vigor to write felt like a confirmation that it was time to speak. I gradually noticed other indicators that felt like winks from God. Multiple trusted people encouraged me on separate occasions to begin speaking up and speaking out. As opportunities arose, the hesitation I felt before was gone.

During my time of silence, I held onto many secrets with God, so I had plenty of ideas to share. I also noticed how my perspective and ways of living had shifted. Instead of immediately dispensing ideas I learned in the quiet place, they quietly transformed my inner world and, slowly, my interactions with the external world. I missed out on the validation of peers in sharing what God taught me in His Word and by His Spirit, but I gained confidence in the changes He created in me.

This chapter started with a nudging moment. I had the idea to write it, then a friend encouraged me that it was time to use my voice. I had made myself a little too comfortable in my time of silence and found myself doubting my voice. Who really needs to hear my thoughts? What makes me so special? Who am I to think I have something to offer? At the end of the day, nothing is new under the sun so why even try?

The nudging continued, so I leaned into it. For better or for worse, our perspectives on reality vary. No one will walk into a room and take it in the way I do or hear a conversation and interpret it the way I will. We may have common consensuses on what matters, but we won't process or store the information in quite the same ways. Our brains are building unique networks throughout our lives to help us comprehend our surroundings. That makes us different. That makes us unique.

This chapter may resonate with you, or it may not. Maybe it does today and won't tomorrow. Ultimately, the results aren't up to me. Obedience is my responsibility; the outcome is God's. Like my mama says, we may never see our legacy on this side of heaven. What matters is that we do the things that He's asked us to do with Him. Isn't that all that matters in life anyway? Our gravestones may hold our legacies, but we hold so much more in our beating hearts today.

LESSON 18

At times, I get so overwhelmed by how dark the world is. Scrolling through the news doesn't take long before we see the brokenness that corrodes our desire for good. Part of my job is to help the local community and partner with local organizations that address specific needs. Have you ever sat across from someone desperately in need and known there's not enough you could do to help them? After you'd done all you could, you'd still be sending them back into a traumatic situation: homelessness, mental diseases, severe addiction, prostitution, neglect.

Earlier this week, I sat in a meeting with a woman who was going home to a husband with explosive anger. That meeting was followed by a teenager on the brink of homelessness. That meeting was followed by a phone call with a mother who struggled to maintain her marriage through postpartum depression. The day ended with a discussion about the food shortage we were dealing with to feed the 40,000 kids in our county trapped in a food desert.

In graduate school, our professors encouraged us to find ways to relax after hearing people talk about their problems all day. Back when my clients only stressed about minor inconveniences and passive comments, it wasn't hard for me to wash the heaviness away with a warm bath. But as the problems escalate, the guilt of returning to a peaceful home doesn't wash off so easily. I try to tell myself I've done all I can do and sit down with a cup of tea but worry eats away at my peace of mind. How can so many people suffer so much? It's not right.

It's not right. And that's when the anger sets in. It's not right! How could someone do *that*? Why can't people be better? When does it end? How could we ever make all these troubles go away? Why do people lie? Why do people take advantage of the systems in place to help them? Then, all of a sudden, I was enraged by the very people I wanted to help. Immediately, the guilt takes over. I know better. People's contexts keep them from thriving. Others don't have the support I had growing up. Some never learned the skills my privileged education afforded me.

Then I feel naive. I've been trying to help, and I know I'm being lied to about some, if not all, of the details of sad stories. There's no way I could understand the complete picture and no way everyone is being transparent. I beg God to purify my heart and fill me with His compassion and wisdom. I know I need it. I remind myself that it's my privilege now to be an instrument of peace where there is chaos. I feel grateful to have any agency at all in these broken situations. But when I look back at my tea, I feel hopeless that I'm not there now. I can do nothing and may never see most of these people again. Did I do enough?

Then I cry at the kitchen counter, and my roommate Cara tells me what I do is amazing, and a step in the right direction. Little acts of kindness matter, and all we can do is what we can do. It's familiar because it's what I tell my friends when they're weighed down by the brokenness that's too cavernous for a handful of passionate people to fill. The words don't bring resolution because I know the ripple effect of my hour-long meeting won't change the tide. But the love behind her words calms the chaos in my heart.

I wait anxiously for my ministry-maintenance therapy session. My therapist and I discuss setting realistic expectations for people I'm trying to help. Maybe they will lie, maybe they won't come back, maybe they're trying to take advantage of the system, maybe they'll take two steps forward, then a giant one back. Love is patient. She challenges my motives. Do I want to help, or do I want to control? Of course, I want to help. But the way I want to help is to control. How fair is taking someone's autonomy when they already lack so much? How arrogant is it to assume I can fix someone's life without having lived in the complexity of it? How counterintuitive is it to disempower the ones in need?

My taste of this experience puts me more in awe of Jesus' ministry on earth and God's wisdom in His covenant with humanity. If you come to my office for a meeting, hardship probably isn't the word that will come to mind as a defining characteristic. My Stanley or Starbucks cup is on the table in an office decorated like a living room with a volcano candle burning. Hypocrisy is subtle but runs deep. I've experienced pain, so it's presumptive to believe I can't relate at all, but you wouldn't be entirely wrong to judge me. My efforts to curate a welcoming and warm environment can be more offensive than soothing.

Jesus chose to make Himself known through suffering. He chose a path of humility, rejection, and persecution. He chose to die for us, knowing the world's brokenness would persist beyond His resurrection. I think He wanted us to know He's not above our pain. He knew betrayal, assault, humiliation, and abandonment.

Jesus could have controlled us into salvation. But He chose patient endurance. He decided to repeat the same truth in a thousand different ways to display the consistency of His character. He allows us to choose restoration. His grace is more than what I sometimes deem responsible for giving away in my finite resources. But He is infinite and generous.

A deep silence of confusion and reverence fills me. He left. He could have stayed, but He left. It's hard for me to understand how Jesus could do that. But He didn't leave us just to leave. He left to send the Holy Spirit to us. He had intention, plans, and care.

I think I would greatly grow by stepping back and letting the Holy Spirit teach, comfort, and advocate.

I feel sad that churches are vilified for not doing enough, for hypocrisy, for failing. You're not wrong if you feel that way. We are failures. It's only the mercy of God that makes us more than we are. I know not every church leader is trying their best. People abuse systems in every system. We need accountability, we need unity, we need humility. But we also need grace. We need partnership. We need Jesus.

We've normalized writing off groups because of individual experiences—iterations of the same sin run through generations: racism, classism, sexism, ableism, etc. Now, when one person at a company says something wrong, we throw the baby out with the bath water. It doesn't matter whether it's a church, shoe company, or sports team. In our pursuit of justice, we've become merciless. In our pursuit of accountability, we've become critical. To protect our mission, we've become preoccupied with protecting our reputation. We forget that we are all a mess. Grace was never meant to excuse our mistakes. Being gracious toward one another is not to dismiss justice and accountability. We've got to think bigger.

I started getting down in the dumps about how great the need is and how far away we are from a solution. A friend did his best to lift my spirit with kind words and sweet treats. All the chaos in me settled as it dawned on me that love matters because love is what lasts. Our whole world is broken, and humanity is prone to selfishness. We're going to keep messing up, keep screwing each other over, keep making tragic decisions in our carelessness or anger. Love is what brings meaning to our existence and our relationships. Love is the thread that runs through our humanity. Love is our hope in the darkness and the purpose of our painful progress. Love is the seed of God we sow into the world as we wait for the garden to bloom. I don't know how to fix the world. I don't even know where to start. But I know God is our Savior, and He is love, so we've got to follow Him in His plans for restoration.

LESSON 19

One year, I did a deep dive on the word *enjoy*. I started a new journal conveniently at the beginning of the year. I decided to break my year up by months and have a mini-theme to help me focus on various aspects of enjoyment. I set themes of enjoying love, God's covering, abundant grace, rest, etc.

During this year, I came about during a particularly rough patch. My therapist agreed to see me weekly for a while, and my friends supported me graciously while I hid away in my room like a hermit. As I approached a new month, I dreaded picking a theme and setting goals.

Along with each theme, I set goals spiritually, emotionally, physically, financially, relationally, and occupationally. My grief severely hindered my natural drive to dream and achieve. Open journal, blank page, I asked the Lord to inspire me with something to fix my mind on for the month.

While my energy levels were depleted and my hopes for the future were low, some things were stable and good. Love, forgiveness, contentment, and other qualities held me together. We can see the product of these, but they are in themselves intangible; they are unseen. As strange as it seemed, I knew I needed to focus on what was unseen.

My confidence grew as I pictured myself clinging to these unseen things for the next month. In a way, it became an opportunity to build my faith. Faith is belief in things we can't see. If there's one thing that can help us through difficult times, it's an assurance of things we hope for and conviction of the unseen. Just like Abraham did not consider the deadness of Sarah's womb when given a promise of offspring and Noah built an ark in a drought, I could choose faith in God over the senselessness of my circumstances.

First, a disclaimer: I don't believe faith *denies* reality. It is a new definition of reality based on the power of God and hope in Christ. I was still sad and grieving. The difference was that my circumstances didn't define my life. The hope of Christ speaks to my identity, pain, and future. I had no idea how to imagine my future. But my confidence grew that God was with me and would continue to be with me all my life. I want Him to do what He wants to do. Faith helps me realign my will with His to bring about the life He has purposed for me.

Love is the easiest of the unseen qualities for me to dwell on. One day, my sister consoled me over the phone as I had a meltdown that could rival her toddler's. She told me grief is an expression of love. Rather than dragging myself through the grief process as an unavoidable evil, I could accept it in remembrance of the love I cherished for so long. There's an element of dignity and beauty to the process of grief despite the tragedy and heaviness of it. Acknowledging the love in the pain helped me feel grateful for my grief. The love we give is never wasted. It may not always be protected, fruitful, or well-expressed, but it is not a waste.

Another unseen quality I felt drawn to was forgiveness. At face value, we can all agree forgiveness is a good thing. But it looks much less enticing when we have to put it into practice. Once forgiveness flows through us, we can't deny the liberating quality.

Forgiving feels like swimming to shore from the middle of the ocean. I try and try but don't seem to get any closer to land. Drowning in my bitterness would be easier, but that's not how I want to go out. I have to trust that eventually, God will send a rescue boat or give me the strength to endure.

Some needs for forgiveness are more apparent than others. The memories that haunt you and the comments you stew on are recognizable places to start. The things we don't want to think about are other places waiting for forgiveness to bring healing. When these come to mind, I tell God I choose to forgive again and ask Him to heal me. I knew I needed to pray through these memories of mine to work out some of the healing. I shut the door to my room and lay in my bed. Closing my eyes, I returned to the memory at its origin and began praying. I recalled one scene, one hurtful word, one scary moment at a time, asking the Lord what He had to say about each part.

During this forgiveness exercise, I felt the Lord recentering my heart on the truth about what He thinks about me and how He loves me. I am His daughter, whom He protects and nurtures. His love is not careless or inconsistent like others I've been wounded by. I also felt the Lord purifying my beliefs about people who have hurt me. They are children of God whom God protects and nurtures. I don't have to fear that hurt will overcome us or that others need me to heal them. God can and will take care of them, too. This exercise in prayer and healing opened up a well of forgiveness in me that I could draw from. After praying through some of these painful events, I found myself exhausted and asked the Holy Spirit to refresh me.

In a mini-miracle, my dad called at that moment. He prayed for me and encouraged me. As we were hanging up, my grandma called and offered her support. I knew it was time to shake off some of the heaviness and let my heart rest. The rest of the day, I walked my dog and casually chatted with friends about other aspects of life. A couple of days later, I finally felt the turn in the tides and was ready to come out of my hole and live again.

I wish I could say I checked off the forgiveness box then and there, but that wouldn't be true. Forgiveness isn't a one-time event. All the consequential disappointments and frustrations from initial painful events also needed to be washed in forgiveness. I would have to choose forgiveness hundreds of times. That forgiveness didn't feel as productive as the other forgiveness exercise, but I believe it is just as much a part of the recovery process. Every time I suffered due to my initial grievance, I had to choose forgiveness. But instead of viewing this as a chore, I started to see it as an opportunity to heal a little more. Every setback moment made me a little closer to whole because I could ask Jesus to fill my brokenness. Skipping an event to avoid someone? Forgive. Leaving work halfway through the day because I couldn't get my emotions under control? Forgive. Missing things from the past? Forgive. Crying alone in my car? Forgive. We endure thousands of painful moments following a painful event that most likely our transgressor never intended. While blaming the people who have wronged us might feel good for a while, it wouldn't *be* good. Forgiveness means releasing the resentment that distorts our enjoyment of life. We have to forgive people for the implications of their mistakes if we want to recover and hope they can work out forgiveness on their end.

Unfortunately, forgiveness is mainly behind the scenes. I have to trust what is done in secret, what is unseen, will lead me closer to God. He is the only One here who can validate the pain we feel and the work we do in our hearts and minds.

I hate living through painful experiences. I hunt for any silver lining to fixate on through the darkest times. The most minor silver lining revealed itself a couple of weeks into this period of grief. The last time I went through significant grief like that was a few years ago. I, undoubtedly, did not handle it well back then. I lost my appetite, lost too much weight, lost my motivation to get better, blamed God, and wore my broken heart on my sleeve everywhere I went. When the Lord finally dragged my stubborn spirit out of the darkness, I soaked in the light. I basked in warm and powerful rays of conviction that He is with me, merciful and kind. I look back on God's graciousness to me as an Ebenezer of His kindness, but I've wondered how I would respond to such pain in the future. Would I have the tools to respond better the next time around? Paul the Apostle once said he learned the secret to being content in every situation. In my last valley, I was not content. Then, back on the mountain tops, I felt a steady stream of contentment in my spirit. I wondered what I would feel when I returned to the valleys.

So far, my contentment has remained. I look back on all I've learned with God over the last few years and see how He's strengthened my trust in Him. Of the numerous painful life events I've endured over the last few years, only one resolved remotely close to how I prayed it would. That one taught me the miraculous power of God. The rest taught me I don't need to have my way to have a life I love. Whether God swings things in my favor or another way, He's staying with me. His faithfulness is the foundation of my contentment. My everlasting life with Love is secure no matter what or who I lose. Am I still pain-avoidant? So far, yes. But I learned the secret Paul gave to us: I can get through anything with God.

This doesn't mean I'm happy all the time. I still ride my waves of emotion. Only now am I content on the emotional rollercoaster. A deeper, still part of my spirit rests underneath the chaos of the storms in life. One exercise that helps me find stillness is meditation on God and His Word. I've grown up meditating since I was a child. My nature was not calm or patient. Meditating slows down my racing mind and raging emotions. Occasionally, I meditate on Scripture or a characteristic of God. Several times now, I've gone through extended commitments to meditating every morning and night for at least ten minutes. This discipline has produced contentment by continually fixing my mind and heart on Jesus. The practice of being still before God daily reaps an undeniable blessing of endurance and enjoyment.

I had a girls' beach trip planned when my grief wave hit. I wasn't at the top of my game. But refreshment filled me by escaping town and feeling the water wash over my feet as I read in the sun. I turned on the saddest playlist I could make on the drive back up, put in my AirPods, and closed my eyes. Heading home to my mess of real life was gut-wrenching. I felt sad for a while, then took out my headphones to rejoin the light conversation with my girlfriends. Much to my surprise, I happened upon a lovely and meaningful chat. They shared what they had learned from one another through their friendships.

Meredith and I became friends in 2015. We lived together for a few years and stayed in touch after moving out of our college town. She was the first solid friend I made at the University of Georgia and one of the first women to teach me the value of strong female friendships.

Meredith teared up in the passenger seat as she told me how beautiful my relationship with God has been to watch grow over the years. She told me how, from her perspective, I should have every reason to rebel against God because of the disappointments and hopes deferred I've endured. But every time I choose God and every time, God comes through for me in some sweet, unique way. She told me how valuable my history with God is and how inspirational my faith has been to her.

I cried, too. This time, from how desperately I had wanted someone to acknowledge my pain and understand my heart. I'm so grateful for that moment. I would've missed out on it if I chose not to go to the beach, if I chose to keep my sad playlist on, or if I didn't have the friendships I have. Those words would have never been said if I hadn't been through hardship or if God weren't the kind of Love who stays through thick and thin. Suppose Meredith wasn't the kind of friend to see people's hearts and be bold enough to say what she sees. I feel God in all the depth of emotion that rushes in moments like that. My history with God and His history of faithfulness to His people keeps my heart content. In disappointment, frustration, and hardship, He is my contentment.

I can't see God. I can't always see His faithfulness. But I know He's there. He is unseen and yet in everything. My faith is in the truth that He will never change, and I will change again and again as I become more assured that I am His. Of all the unseen things in existence, God is by far the most beautiful of them all. He will always be there to keep me going.

LESSON 20

As a chronic people-pleaser, I am so scared of disappointing my people. I think many people my age are more afraid of disappointing people than angering them. We grew up in the "I'm not mad, just disappointed" generation, which left a mark on me. Fearing abandonment only exacerbates my fear of disappointing someone. I've worked myself up to believe that they'll leave me if I don't live how my people expect me to.

My friend Hope disavowed me of these notions. She told me that she may occasionally be disappointed in the decisions I make for my life, but she wouldn't leave me over them. She would voice her concerns but wouldn't bail on our friendship. I wouldn't bail on a friendship over a disagreement, either. Strangely enough, it wasn't until I heard Hope say it out loud that I realized other people might have similar values for friendship. Especially at this age with friendships that have lasted this long, I don't know how I could've believed my friends didn't love me as much as I love them.

I've had too many friendships that fizzled out with moves, changing schools, and changing jobs, and I started wrongly assuming nobody could love me enough to stick around. Rather than believing these were natural life transitions, I took the loss personally. It's nice to be wrong sometimes.

My friends have shown me love is self-controlled, trusting, hopeful, and persevering. They've chosen to be a part of my life through my best and worst decisions. I have a good feeling it will take a lot for our hearts to turn against each other.

Americans aren't especially great at communal living. We're individualistic at best and self-focused more often. In my travels, I've seen other cultures embrace collectivism and close relationships much better. Visiting other countries showed me I adhered to the Western ideals of individualism and needed to find my way back to balance between individuality and collectivism.

I like being independent, ambitious, and strong. But a lot of the bravado is the external shell I've built around the core of me that wants to be cared for, fought for, and believed in. To get the love I need, I will have to let people past my external shell. At times, I'll need to put the needs of others above my own.

Recently, I learned about Jews in ancient times and how God set laws to govern their interactions. You've heard "eye for an eye" from their customs. They had extensive and oddly specific laws to protect enslaved people, women, and people in poverty. Everyone in the community was, to some degree, responsible for themselves and the well-being of others.

I've spent so long concerned about the responsibility for myself that I blocked off others from investing in my well-being. The truth is, I still need my mom to mother me. I still need my dad to protect me. I need my siblings to goof off with me and my friends to explore the world with me. I need mentors to guide me and pastors to disciple me. I still need a partner to share life with me.

I don't need these things like I need food and shelter, a job, or good health. But I need them like I need beauty and belonging. I realized I'd been running so far down a track to prove myself that I outran the people I wanted to share life with.

The scary thing about communal living is the division of power. You can't just do your own thing at your own pace and hope for the best. You have to consider the impact of your life on the people who depend on you. You have to choose the people to trust and trust the people you choose. You have to have grace for one another, hope for the future, gratefulness for the ones who surround you, and forgiveness for the ones who hurt you.

I joke that my life is a sitcom, but it's not that easy. We don't all meet at someone's apartment daily to hang out or have a deli shop we frequent. We don't date each other or enable codependency to further the plot. We're not all in our late twenties trying to make the most of life before the big, dreaded thirty. Most of my people live in different cities, even other states. We have various opinions about God, though we all believe He loves us. Our strongest values aren't all the same, though they're compatible. We all have different backgrounds and upbringings.

The bond that holds us together is love for one another and trust in God. These are people I can depend on and trust. They're the ones who hear about the big moments first and don't mind wasting time in moments that don't mean anything other than that we want to be together. We live to become our best and love the people around us the best we can.

In a recent therapy session, I was advised to take two weeks off from analyzing a problem I faced and instead ask my people to pray on my behalf. They could share anything they felt strongly about while praying for me, but other than that, I wouldn't think about the problem at hand. I'd just relax and recover my life outside of the problem. I contacted about ten people I trusted, and everyone spent intentional time praying and sending me what they prayed about.

Those two weeks were the most enjoyable I had spent in a while. I felt free to breathe and see the world with a new perspective. I felt the pressure fall off my shoulders and didn't waste all my mental energy on the same problem daily. It was almost like a vacation from my life without actually going anywhere. I'd wake up every day wondering what I wanted to fill my days with since I had no significant problems to solve.

At the end of the two weeks, I compiled all the prayers and thoughts of the people I had asked and spent quiet time sorting through them. I don't know why I was so shocked. My people all came through for me. I don't know when my trust in people crashed so low. But this built my faith in others back up. It's amazing how much peace, clarity, and creativity flood our minds when we believe we are loved and accepted. I felt like I could do anything. I'd take one text or conversation at a time and pray, "Lord, do you have anything to say about this today?" Then, I waited for insight and wrote down what resonated in me.

Once I decided between God and me what I wanted to do, I called my checkpoint people. These people know me the best, and I trust them to tell me if I'm off. Again, I was surprised by the love and care I felt even when I was being cautioned and corrected. My checkpoint people didn't all give the same response to my decision.

Some agreed with me wholeheartedly; others voiced their hesitations alongside their support for me. The point of talking with them wasn't for approval or permission; it was for perspective.

As a twenty-something-year-old, I feel like I know so much. It's hard to accept sometimes that I don't know everything. It kind of hurts my pride. But there is a way to know more than I know: to let people help me. I can ask people what they see that I'm not seeing or what they see that I'm not giving enough attention to. With a mix of trusted people and trusted opinions, I can broaden my perspective and ask the Lord for discernment in what to emphasize.

One of my most significant raw spots is how sensitive I am. I used to resent it, but now I'm working on it. I can be easily overwhelmed. With such a great group of checkpoint people, I can get maxed out on input. These people know that about me and have grace for my weakness. When I tell them I don't want to talk about something anymore, or I'm not ready to hear any more opinions, they respect that. Love is patient, and these people are the best at being patient with me.

Even writing this, I felt emotional and grateful for the fantastic people I have in my corner. It's taken years to cultivate, and some of the main characters in my story have traded out over the seasons. But here's what I believe: if it can happen for me, it can happen for you. I hope you find the Pa to your Half-Pint, the Mary-Kate to your Ashley, the March sisters to your Teddy, the Avengers to your Black Widow, and the Simon to your Garfunkel. With them and with God, you can sail over troubled waters. You can persevere to the very ends of the earth.

As I finish this book with a grateful heart, I acknowledge the goodness of God to give me this life and people to enjoy it with. I hope you can look around with gratitude for the life you've been cultivating as well. At the very least, I pray you can look to the horizon with hope. Whether on stormy or still waters, you're not alone in the boat. Jesus is God with us. Whether He is silent or silencing the storms, He keeps you safe. I hope these lessons encourage you like they did for me as you sail on.

ABOUT THE AUTHOR

Savannah is a storyteller, weaving narratives of faith, resilience, and connection seamlessly together. With her debut book, "For My Girls," she captured the hearts of her readers, offering reflections on loving God, yourself, and others. Now, with her second release, "Sail On," Savannah continues to inspire with a compelling blend of personal testimony and biblical insight.

As a young pastor with six years of dedicated ministry service, Savannah brings a fresh perspective to the age-old themes of perseverance and steadfastness in the face of life's trials. Drawing from her experiences and the timeless truths of Scripture, Savannah offers precious insights and practical wisdom for navigating seas of adversity with hope, peace, and unwavering trust in God. Her lessons give solace to the weary soul and illuminate the path toward spiritual renewal.

Made in the USA
Columbia, SC
21 July 2024

38487470R00085